Alain
BAXTER

For James, Bella, Joan & Alf

Alain
BAXTER

•◆ Andrew Ross

dewi lewis media ltd

Alain BAXTER
By Andrew Ross

© 2005 For this edition: Dewi Lewis Media Ltd
© 2005 For the text: Andrew Ross
© 2005 For the photographs: Graeme Hunter, Aviemore Photographic,
Pavel Satny, Stewart Easson and the Baxter and Dickson Families

This edition first published in the UK in November 2005 by
Dewi Lewis Media Ltd
8, Broomfield Road
Heaton Moor
Stockport SK4 4ND
www.dewilewismedia.com

> Original Design Concept
Arco da Velha – Design e Ilustração, Lda, Portugal. Based on the design
originally conceived for the book 'José Mourinho: Made in Portugal'

> Artwork Production
Dewi Lewis Media Ltd

> Print and binding
Biddles Ltd, Kings Lynn

ISBN: 0-9546843-5-4

12   11   10   9   8   7   6   5   4   3   2   1

Front Cover Photograph of Alain Baxter by Graeme Hunter
Author Photograph of Andrew Ross by Stewart Easson

>> **CONTENTS**

> INTRODUCTION   **7**

> PROLOGUE   **11**

> LIVING THE DREAM   **15**

> A FAMILY STORY   **35**

> TESTING TIMES   **55**

> STARTING OUT   **75**

> THE FIGHT BEGINS   **99**

> UP THE RANKINGS   **119**

> FACING A BAN   **139**

> UNCHARTED WATERS   **159**

> THE APPEAL   **179**

> MOVING ON   **199**

INTRODUCTION

ALAIN BAXTER

Andrew Ross

INTRODUCTION

I first met Alain Baxter in the summer of 2004. I'd travelled to the remote Scottish village of Aviemore to meet and interview the elusive skier. Baxter was late, but when he did arrive the figure standing in front of me bore no resemblance to the ambitious athlete who had thrown caution to the wind to clinch an historic Olympic bronze medal in Salt Lake City in 2002. He is Britain's only Olympic skiing medallist.

Baxter was shy, guarded and suspicious – his stock response to journalists since he was sensationally, and unjustly, stripped of his medal shortly after the Games. But as he relaxed, the real Baxter emerged: a modest and introverted character, highly dedicated to his sport at the expense of everything else, punctuality included. He has been known to keep reporters waiting for hours while he completes his gruelling daily six-hour training regime. His dedication to improvement through sheer hard graft beggars belief.

It was to be the first of many meetings. The magazine interview never materialised, instead the germ of a plan to put together a book about Baxter's amazing journey from penniless schoolboy living in a caravan with no electricity or running water, to top ten skier, standing on the Olympic podium, before being unceremoniously stripped of the prize.

Persuading Baxter to participate in the book was harder than convincing a publisher to take a chance on it. For the latter, the attraction was clear. Baxter's story is the great untold British sporting tale. The story of a boy battling non-stop for fifteen years against the odds, against the near-insurmountable financial constraints, to emerge at the top of the pile of 6,000 international ski racers. It would be a fairytale but for the terrible twist of fate which befell the honest skier (more of that inside).

Baxter initially refused to get involved in the project. His reasoning – that it would be too much of a diversion from his unrelenting training regime in the run up to the 2006 Winter Olympics. Baxter was also suspicious that the author was unscrupulously seeking to profit from the explosive and highly controversial nature of his story. He was right, in part. It was a once-in-a-lifetime opportunity for a young writer to chance upon an athlete whose name everyone knows but whose fate few are familiar with.

But there was no reason to dress-up or exaggerate what Baxter has lived through. The truth is far more staggering than any fiction could be.

Over time Baxter was won over but he had three conditions. Firstly, that there was to be absolutely no disruption to his training schedule. This would lead to the author spending hours with the skier in gyms, on long bike rides, in expensive telephone conversations between the UK and Argentina, and, inevitably, sitting on his doorstep in Aviemore for hours on end wondering where the hell he was (he'd be doing extra training). What started as a hindrance, soon proved to be a unique opportunity to observe a world class athlete in his true environment.

Baxter's second condition for doing the book was that it would be honest. He'd never given a full account of the doping scandal which had engulfed him after the 2002 Olympics and it was agreed that the book would, for once and for all, tell the real story of what happened. Baxter warned me that he would not enjoy retelling the events which caused him and his family so much hurt, which have tainted his reputation forever, but when the time came he was brutally honest and frank. There was no attempt to sugar-coat it. The result, I hope, is a fascinating and exclusive insight into the mind of one of our nation's true unsung heroes.

Baxter's final condition was that the book would not focus solely on the doping scandal. I agreed to this condition with the intention of later breaking the promise if necessary. There'd be no need. As Baxter took me on a journey from the nursery slopes of the Cairngorm Mountains – via countless nights spent sleeping in his car in the Alps as he pursued his dream – to the World Cup Slalom slopes of Kitzbuehel in front of 60,000 screaming fans, it became apparent that there was so much more to the Scotsman's story than meets the eye.

Baxter's story is unique, yet the themes are universal. His story is not just for winter sports fanatics. It is inspiring. It is of a young boy daring to dream the impossible and of achieving it against the odds. It is about the triumph of human spirit in the face of incalculable adversity. And most of all, it is about unfinished business.

Andrew Ross
October, 2005, London

PROLOGUE

PROLOGUE

It had taken Scottish skier Alain Baxter fifteen years of hard work, fifteen years of sacrifice. Now, finally, the skier known as 'The Highlander' stood at the top of the Salt Lake Olympic Slalom course at Deer Valley, Utah, preparing to take on the cream of the world's skiers.

He was unique, as a Brit, to find himself at the start of a world class race with a genuine chance of making the podium. It was what Baxter had always dreamed of since taking his first tentative run on skis in the Scottish Highlands as a child. He wasn't going to waste his golden opportunity.

To put into context the magnitude of what he was about to undertake it is worth considering that more Britons have been in space than have won Olympic skiing medals. All the obscure statistics in the world couldn't mask the cold, hard truth that, as Baxter was about to tackle the most technical and demanding of all the Alpine Skiing disciplines, Britain had never, in the 78 year history of the Winter Games, had a skier on the podium.

Standing in the starter's tent at the top of the daunting Slalom course on a stormy morning on February 23, 2002, Baxter waited as he watched skier after skier go out of the gate to embark on their first of, hopefully, two runs. Normally, the Scot would have preferred to stay focused on his own performance, travelling the course in his mind, like a Formula 1 driver memorising the corners of a race track. But at Deer Valley the wait was unavoidable. From the tent, the remaining skiers were forced to watch their rivals negotiate the first fifteen gates of the challenging course before disappearing over a steep pitch into the unknown.

The nerves and excitement of the starting gate were not new to Baxter, nor was the prospect of posting a good result in a world class field. But to do so with the world's media watching on was a new experience. The statisticians had done their work, however. Starting 20th out of 76 racers (based on World Ranking), Baxter could expect a top twenty finish, at best.

Baxter was nothing if not a pragmatist. Knowing what a lottery the slalom could be, he knew that he had a good chance to significantly improve his position from the first run. He knew, too, that he had to break into the top fifteen on his first run or have no chance of a medal whatsoever. The odds were stacked against Baxter, as they had been throughout his career, but he was a natural competitor and had waited so many years for this moment to arrive.

It had been perfect skiing conditions all week in Salt Lake running up to the Slalom, the blue riband event of the Games. But when Baxter awoke on the day of the biggest race of his life he was greeted by a familiar sight – at least one very familiar to a Scot. There was wind, snow, rain, and fluctuating temperatures and snow conditions – just like a normal day at Baxter's home slope in Aviemore. The conditions didn't prey too heavily on the mind of the Highlander as he stood at the start gate, waiting for the green light. If the weather conditions were an omen, it was one wasted on the determined Scotsman. The conditions were bad for everyone.

Now it was down to who wanted it the most...

> CHAPTER I   **LIVING THE DREAM**

OUT OF THE STARTING GATE
A SENSE OF DISAPPOINTMENT
IT'S GETTING BETTER ALL THE TIME
THE FIRST BRITON EVER
REALITY DAWNS
THE HERO RETURNS

1   LIVING THE DREAM

"The starter gave the signal. I paused for a second to compose my thoughts, then pushed forward and flew out of the start gate. It was the perfect start, but because it was quite flat I had ten or fifteen gates to really get going, to put the hammer down and flow. In other races when the start is steeper I can get quite passive and negative in my style, but here it was perfect.

"I remember thinking, 'This is OK. Keep this up. Don't hold back over the pitch.' There was a Banana gate * coming onto the pitch so I just wanted to keep going, on the outside ski. It started to get really bumpy but I did exactly what I had in my mind: stood on the outside ski, moved forward and accelerated through the gates in one motion.

"Further down, there were a couple of really close calls. I hit bumps, lost my balance, almost straddled a gate, but I kept going and didn't lose my momentum. I fought to the last gate and when I got down and saw my time I was pleased. I was 8th and I knew from the difficulty of the course that there weren't going to be seven guys coming down and beating me."

Baxter was right. He would start the second run safely in the middle of the top 15, just where he'd wanted to be. And, with the unforgiving course for the first run putting paid to the Olympic dreams of 26 of the 76 starters, including all four Italian skiers and two of the hotly-tipped Austrian team, Baxter's dream of getting on the podium inched marginally closer to reality.

"In racing, starting the second run in 8th is pretty perfect, if a little too far out to challenge for the podium. I was two seconds off the lead, which in good conditions would have been too much to make up. But the conditions were in my favour. If I took the risk and went for it in the second run anything could happen."

As Baxter crossed the line after his first run you could have been forgiven for thinking he was racing in front of a home crowd in the windswept Cairngorm Mountains, such was the support. Enthusiastic locals had joined with the handful of friends and family who had made the long trip to cheer

---

* A Banana gate is a double gate turning in the same direction, enabling the racer to ski through in one long curve

on The Highlander. Among their number was Baxter's cousin, Lesley McKenna, who had competed in the Snowboard Half-pipe competition, and Janis Baxter, the mother of Baxter's half-brother Noel, a promising young skier who was also competing in the Slalom. An ex-international skier herself, McKenna knew her older cousin would be pleased with his first run. However, not everyone shared her view.

"I knew Alain would have been excited because he had given himself a great platform to challenge for a medal. That was something we had dreamed about since we were children and I was desperate to find him and congratulate him. While going up to find him a British skiing journalist said to me, 'That won't be good enough will it?' I told him to save his breath for when Alain won a medal."

The reporter's pessimism was one shared by host broadcaster, NBC. Fiona McNeilly, Operations Director of the British Ski and Snowboard Federation (BSSF), had been negotiating with NBC and the BBC to decide who would interview Baxter first after the race. McNeilly admits to being more nervous than Baxter before his final run, sensing a truly historic result.

"If Alain could ski down even into the top ten it would be a massive result for British skiing. In this event BBC would take precedence and it didn't take much to persuade NBC that this was the case. They seemed quite laissez faire about the whole thing, assuming that a podium place was out of reach."

Far away from Salt Lake millions of television viewers awaited Baxter's second run with baited breath. For the first time televisions in British pubs were showing skiing not football. After the gold medal success of the British Curling team, the embers of Olympic fever burnt on in the UK and many tuned in to hear Graham Bell, the last British skier to grab the headlines, commentate on Alain's race.

With his job done a shy Baxter eluded the waiting press pack and headed for the chairlift. There, he bumped into Mathias Berthold a former coach who he credited with taking him from the verge of quitting the sport in 1996 to breaking through into the top 100 some two years later.

"Mathias was head coach of the Austrian Women's Ski team. I met him as he stepped off the chairlift but he was in a hurry. We'd had an old saying from the first time I'd ever qualified for the World Championships. We'd arrived the night before the race and Mathias said to me, 'OK Alain, let's win the medal and f**k off!' And that was exactly what he shouted after me as I got on the chairlift."

Baxter's first run had not only grabbed the attention of old friends. In the food hall as Baxter ate alone, meditating on the second run, an agent for one of the major ski manufacturers approached him and enquired whether he was in the market for a new sponsorship deal. It was an unwelcome diversion for Baxter who has a reputation for hating the frippery that surrounds being a professional athlete. He was there to race, nothing else, but this type of approach would be a taste of things to come if Baxter could pull off the biggest result in British Olympic history.

After lunch Baxter went up to inspect the course set for the second run. It was slightly different to the first in that it took skiers straight over the steep pitch as opposed to across it. Skiing conditions, if anything, were even more unforgiving than they had been in the morning. Anyone who was going to win a medal that afternoon was going to have to earn it.

Back in the start area Baxter talked through the course with coach Christian Schwaiger. As he warmed-up and tension mounted as the first skiers made their way to the start gate, the experienced Austrian gave Baxter his final briefing:

"You can approach this in two ways. You could take it easy and move up a couple of places if you are lucky, or you can go for it, for the podium. That's why we're here isn't it? You've got nothing to lose so don't be afraid to take a few risks."

Baxter nodded in agreement. Schwaiger made it sound easy, so within reach, but inside the Scot knew the enormity of the task. To win a medal he would have to ski at the limit. He'd have to risk crashing out unceremoniously, to make up the two seconds on the leader. As those starting ahead of him filtered out, Baxter soon found himself in the starter's tent again, knowing that the next 50 seconds could change his life forever.

"I watched a couple of guys go through the first section of the course. There were seven who went before me and a couple crashed out. It was a reality check. They hadn't crashed because the course was more difficult than in the morning. It was because this was the Olympic Games and we were all two seconds or more down on the leaders. It was all or nothing.

"On the final run my aim was just to make up the two seconds. I'd gone quick in the first run and not many people had made up as many places as me. I knew that if there was any chance whatsoever of getting a medal I'd have to risk everything. I don't usually get that nervous before a race. You've got to be fired up but relaxed too. It's a balance. If you're too aggressive you can go out on the first gate, which is useless. But I knew I had to go for it. I also knew that the course was in good condition. Few of the skiers ahead of me had made it past the pitch so I knew the course would be pristine further down.

"Christian was trying not to get me too hyped-up but I knew what I had to do. He'd done his job in the months running up to the Games. France's Sebastian Amiez, who had recorded an identical time to mine (50.16 seconds) in the first run, went before me. I saw the start of his run and he looked good. Forty seconds later I heard the tannoy announcing that he'd gone into the lead. Twenty seconds after he'd finished it was my turn.

It would be a massive result for British skiing

"I put my sticks over the wand. The starter said, 'Ready, go!' It was now or never. I thought about the race for a few seconds, got myself fired up, and lunged forward out of the gate. I gave myself a couple of pushes and got into the rhythm. It was the best feeling in the world. I was negotiating the course with ease. I didn't have to think about anything, I didn't have to force any movements, everything came naturally, it was flowing. I remember picking up speed across the flat, coming over the pitch and just loving it. I was putting everything into it but it was so much smoother than the first run. There were no recoveries, I was pinning every gate.

"Conditions were different from the first run – quite similar to Scotland actually – rutted, icy and grippy. I remember coming into a little side hill at the finish. There were four gates into a verticale * then another four gates and the finish. I came into the first four gates on the side hill and I didn't quite nail it. I slid a little bit, carved, slid, carved, slid and then into the verticale. I cursed myself, 'Damn it Baxter!'

"It was straight from there, into the verticale and onto the finish where I looked at the big screen and saw that I was in second place. I was out of

* A verticale is where two tight gates are set vertically above each other

breath, leaning on the safety barrier looking up at the board. I was half a second behind Amiez, but knew deep down that it wasn't going to be enough to stay in the medals. There were still seven of the world's best skiers to come and the notion that at least two of them wouldn't beat me seemed far-fetched."

A SENSE OF DISAPPOINTMENT

Despite the inward disappointment, Baxter was still staring in the face of an historic result. He could be no worse than 9th, an astonishing performance for any skier, let alone a Brit. But this was the Olympics. He'd had a shot at a medal and he'd blown it. As he took off his skis and hoisted them in the air to salute his small band of travelling supporters, Baxter knew immediately that it was those four gates into the verticale that had cost him a medal. As he picked out his cousin and friends in the crowd, a slow motion replay of Baxter's run was played on the big screen, focusing on the section that had slowed the skier. Watching it, Baxter cursed himself again, 'Damn it, there goes my chance of a medal!'

Baxter's gut feeling was right. At this level of skiing seven skiers could easily squeeze into a half second gap. Resigned, and disappointed, Baxter proceeded to the marshal's tent to have his equipment measured. He greeted Amiez there but from the look on his face Baxter could see that he wasn't holding out for a medal either. While Baxter had his skis and boots examined, unbeknown to him, his medal hopes were improving. The two skiers following Baxter had both failed to beat his time. From 9th place he was looking at no worse than 7th. As Baxter retrieved his skis he was joined by McNeilly who'd been watching events unfold with increasing excitement.

"I knew Alain would have been disappointed not to have come down in 1st but he was still looking at a top ten result, which was phenomenal. While I waited for him I watched the last seven from the top group come down. One by one they were either slower than Alain or crashing. There was one racer per minute. That's how quick it was happening. I was thinking, 'Now he can't be worse than 8th... now he can't be worse than 7th...

"Alain was still nowhere to be seen but he joined me soon after and said, 'Wait a minute, what number are we on?' I think that the penny was starting to drop."

There were five skiers from the top group left to go. The legendary Croatian, Ivica Kostelic, was going well until he clipped one of the final gates. Then Slovenia's Mitja Kunc crashed too. Baxter was still second, with three to go. Any earlier ambivalence he'd harboured about the result was quickly evaporating.

IT'S GETTING BETTER ALL THE TIME

"When Kjetil Andre Aamodt, who'd won more Olympic medals than any other skier, came down a second slower than me that was when I first started paying attention. Within minutes there were just two skiers to go, Bode Miller and Jean-Pierre Vidal. I couldn't be worse than 4th but it all happened so quickly that it hadn't really sunk in.

"Bode came flying out of the start gate and the home crowd went wild. He was looking good. I could feel that medal ebb away but in the mid-section he missed a gate completely and went flying past it. Somehow he managed to stay in the course and started side-stepping back up the hill to make the gate. It was excruciating to watch and it took a moment to realise what was happening, that he'd lost too much time. I was definitely in the medals no matter what Vidal did! It was just a question of silver or bronze. I couldn't believe it because I'd already written it off. Top ten would have been a great result but suddenly I had an Olympic medal!"

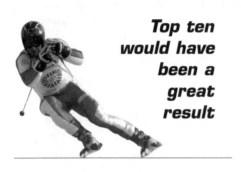

Top ten would have been a great result

McNeilly will never forget Baxter's reaction:

"We were walking toward the BBC reporter when Miller came out of the start gate. We watched on the big screen as he ran wide on the mid-section. Alain didn't react at all. There were no yells, no expletives, as Miller hiked back up to make the gate. Alain's jaw just dropped and his eyes nearly popped out of their sockets. That's my abiding image of the Games."

McKenna has her own memory of the historic moment:

"When Bode messed-up there was a pause before everyone realised what Alain had done. Then the crowd went crazy. It was the best thing I've ever seen. It validated all the effort that any British skier or coach had ever put in, in the distant hope that they would reach the pinnacle of the sport. Suddenly anything was possible."

John Clark, McKenna's team manager and a lifelong friend of Baxter, shared her opinion.

"The most prominent emotion for me was relief. Relief that we hadn't been kidding ourselves all this time that we could actually get someone to compete with the best. A lot of people involved in British skiing thought, 'Thank God we haven't been banging our heads against a brick wall for all these years for nothing.' It meant we were right all along, that we could get someone up there with the elite."

The joy and disbelief were widespread. Graham Bell, who knew how hard Baxter had worked to get where he was, was teary-eyed as he confirmed the result live on the BBC. Vidal had skied down safely into the lead. It was bronze for Baxter. The commentator on NBC summed up the shock that the British skier had caused:

"And in third place... Alain Baxter... of Britain... of all places!"

THE FIRST BRITON EVER

In the blink of an eye Baxter had taken his place in the record books as the first and only British Olympic skiing medallist. With Baxter's result confirmed, McNeilly had a job on her hands getting him past NBC to the BBC. Her phone was ringing off the hook and the pair were soon engulfed by well-wishers and press alike.

"Christian, who's quite a serious character, came running over and put his hand out to shake mine. I said, 'For god's sake Christian, give me a hug.' There was lots of dancing around. Roberto Brunner, Alberto Tomba's ex-manager, now manager of the Austrian Team, came over and gave Alain a big hug too, even though none of his team were in the medals. We also met Sarah Lewis, who was a former boss of mine at the BSSF and who was now second in command at skiing's governing body, FIS. She had tears in her eyes, which was an uncharacteristically partisan act for someone in her position. I knew then that this was going to be massive for Alain, massive for the Federation, and massive for Britain."

While media and friends clambered to congratulate the shy medal winner, Olympic officials arrived to escort him back to the finishing area. Someone threw a Union Jack at Baxter which he hoisted skywards to give the photographers the perfect photo opportunity. Baxter was then whisked back to face the world's press. What he'd achieved had still not sunk in and he had no ready-prepared soundbite for the press. It was the part of his profession that he loathed most but he went from reporter to reporter, even giving an interview in broken German as his confidence grew. But his wide grin and dazed expression spoke volumes. The magnitude of what he'd achieved was only slowly dawning on him as he formulated responses to questions he hadn't even asked of himself.

What happened next typified how unaffected Baxter was, even in his moment of glory. When he heard brother Noel's name on the tannoy he stopped an interview mid-sentence and fled from the press pack to watch his brother complete his second run. Out of contention, Noel formed part of the slower group of skiers who had waited until the fastest fifteen had raced-off to decide the medals. He skied down into a creditable 21st place but instead of finishing in a tight tuck to gain valuable seconds, the younger Baxter crossed the line with his poles aloft in celebration. He'd known before he even got to the start gate that Baxter had won a medal. It was later said that Noel would have snowploughed straight down the piste if it meant he would get to his brother quicker. It was clear that whereas some sportsmen feel alone and peerless in the moment of victory, Baxter's success would be shared by all who knew him. In Edinburgh, Baxter's mother Sue celebrated with family members after taking a brief call from her son: "What about that mum!" In Aviemore, Baxter's father Ian was taking calls from his son's many friends and his ex-coaches. In the Cairngorm Hotel in Aviemore hundreds of supporters celebrated and Baxter's homecoming parade was already being plotted by owner Peter Steinlhe.

Later, back at the Salt Lake media centre, the press pack was even bigger than it had been on the piste. The majority of the British press had not made the 40 minute trip from Salt Lake City to nearby Park City for Baxter's race on the slopes of Deer Valley. Expectations were low and, as it was the last day of the Games, most were packing for flights home that evening. Or so they thought. Newspaper editors in the UK were frantically calling their reporters, cancelling their flights home and relaying the news that Baxter-mania was already gripping the nation. Britain would wake up the next morning to hundreds and hundreds of column inches dedicated to 'The Highlander'.

Journalists of all nationalities were firing questions at Baxter at the conference. Aside from the fact that there were two Frenchmen, and no Austrians or Americans, on the podium, Baxter was the big story. People were asking about his background, about how it felt to come from nowhere to clinch a medal? Baxter spent most time answering the latter.

"Lots of skiers took a risk today and didn't make it. There's a lot that can go wrong in Slalom but I took the risk and made it. This is something I've been training for all my life. It's one of the things that has paid off. Remember, I had a great season last year, and lots of people made me favourite for the

World Championships. I started off pretty badly this season, however, and came here as an outsider. But all my training has been rewarded and it's a great day for British skiing."

After the press conference Baxter went directly to the doping centre to give his mandatory sample. Having not been to the bathroom for hours Baxter had no trouble providing the requisite amount of urine. Indeed, he requested a larger container once he'd done so and continued to urinate for some time before a bemused official. In the relative calm of the testing area Baxter went over the day's events in his head. He still couldn't grasp what he'd achieved and was in a daze. More than anything, Baxter wanted to get the formalities over so he could meet up with friends to celebrate properly.

Noel Baxter

Coming out of the doping area Baxter met the Austrian skier Benjamin Raich, who had finished fourth. The poor performance of the Austrian skiers was viewed as a national disaster for the ski-obsessed nation. Countrymen Killian Albrecht, Rainer Schoenfelder and Raich could easily have recorded a 1-2-3 and no-one would have batted an eyelid. Having two Frenchman and a Brit on the podium had sent shockwaves through the sport. Raich was gracious in defeat, however, and heartily congratulated Baxter.

On the drive back to the team condo in Park City, Baxter made numerous calls to family and friends. It brought him back down to earth and he would have given anything to be transported home that night to join the celebrations in Aviemore. Things were already reaching fever pitch in the small Highland village.

"The celebrations were like Christmas, Hogmanay and Burn's Night all rolled into one," one local would later tell *The Sun*.

With the medal ceremony beckoning, Baxter barely had time to enjoy a quick beer with his brother and the rest of the team before changing into his official Team GB kit, bar the woolly hat that British Olympic Association (BOA) Press Officer Philip Pope insisted he wore. McNeilly joined Baxter and Pope for the journey back down to Salt Lake. Despite being at his side since winning the medal, she had barely uttered a word to the skier since the race.

"On the way to the ceremony I tried to explain to Alain how proud of him I was. Of what a big, big difference this was going to make for the Federation. It was going to change everything, for him, for the team, for the funding. Alain was very team-spirited and said, 'I'll do anything if it helps the team, Fiona.'"

Prior to the medal ceremony Pope had corralled the British press together at their own makeshift media centre – The Dead Goat Saloon. Pope had taken the Curlers there after their triumph, but it was remarked that Baxter seemed most at ease in the down-at-heel bar. From there it was straight on to the ceremony where Baxter would reap the reward of all those years living out of a suitcase, sleeping in the back of his rusted car in sub-zero temperatures, and putting up mile upon mile of fencing during the summers to fund his dream.

No-one could ever take that away from him

Curiously, Baxter's first real opportunity to be alone with his thoughts didn't come until he was standing on the podium. In the moments as he surveyed the crowd, waiting for his fellow medallists to join him, it finally sunk in. He had actually won an Olympic medal and no-one could ever take that away from him.

On the podium Baxter still seemed remarkably calm from the exterior. Not a natural extrovert, it took all the photographers' powers of persuasion to even get him to kiss the medal. But Baxter tried to avoid the glare of the camera flashes as he searched the crowd in vain for familiar faces to share the moment with. It was only when he stepped off the podium that he saw Noel's mother, Janis, and threw his bouquet of flowers to her. The flowers would later be dried and presented to Baxter's grandmother, mother, aunts, and cousins as a lasting reminder of the day he was crowned the best British skier in history.

With all the formalities over it was time for the team to party. Baxter, still in Team GB tracksuit, led the way, eager to enjoy his first drink in weeks. Joined by his coach, physio, ski serviceman and numerous members of the BOA entourage, Baxter decamped to a nearby club. All Baxter's peers and rivals were there and he was humbled on more than one occasion by their comments.

It meant a lot coming from a fellow skier

"In the toilets I met one of the Norwegians. He said to me, 'Of all the guys out there who could have won, I'm glad it was you. You did a good job and you deserve it.' I was chuffed. It meant a lot coming from a fellow skier. Only they could truly understand what it took to compete at this level."

Back out in the bar, enjoying a drink with the team, Baxter was clearly glowing with pride. To be commended by his peers meant everything to the Scot. McNeilly recalls the look on his face when Olympic legend Kjetil Andre Aamodt made a grand entrance wearing a tailored suit which put Baxter's team tracksuit to shame.

"Aamodt arrived looking really dapper. When Alain saw him he nudged me and said, 'I beat him today!'"

Baxter was having the time of his life in the bar. Men's magazine *FHM* was due to host a party there later and all his friends from the ski scene were there, but someone was missing. Noel Baxter, not yet 21, had been refused entry to the club. No amount of persuasion or sheer bribery would change the doorman's mind so, despite it being the biggest night of his life, Baxter left the group and drove back up to the more laid-back surroundings of Park City with brother Noel and cousin Lesley, where they'd be able to celebrate together. Back at the club the party raged on, with few even noticing until much later that the guest of honour was nowhere to be seen.

Family was everything to Baxter and he didn't dwell for long on what he was missing. In Park City they met up with the British Bobsledders and the team doctors and drank on late into the night in a shabby 'All-you-can-drink' bar. McKenna remembers the night fondly:

"It was a special moment to sit with my two cousins talking about all the ridiculous things we'd done in the past to enable us to be there, especially in the context of Alain having just won a medal. Noel was getting very emotional, far more than Alain ever did. He was saying, 'This is for granny and grandad.' It was moving to see how much it meant to him."

The night ended at 6.30am back at McKenna's condo where the three leapt off the balcony into the pool below to find that it wasn't heated and had a thin layer of ice floating just below the surface. A few more leaps in his underwear and the bronze medallist and his brother called it a night. Baxter finally closed his eyes on the best day of his life at 7.30am. He was tired but still excited. It had been a day like no other but he eventually drifted off into a fitful slumber before being rudely awakened an hour later.

REALITY DAWNS

"There was a loud knock at the door at 8.30am. I was disoriented and didn't know what was happening. Then someone burst in with a film crew. I had slept naked, and had only had about an hour's sleep so I wasn't looking too hot. It took a moment to realise that it was Philip Pope. He was there to take me to another press conference. I got up, had a quick shower, put some clothes on and was about to leave when I thought, 'Sh*t, where's the medal?' I panicked but after five frantic minutes searching I remembered that Noel had had it late the night before. I found him sleeping on the couch. I shook him and said, 'Noel, where's the medal?' He wasn't happy. He said: 'What medal? Leave me alone,' and went back to sleep."

The film crew watched on in amusement. Pope was more concerned. There was no question of turning up at the photocall without the medal. The organisation had waited the better part of a century to win a skiing medal and it wasn't going to waste the valuable public relations opportunity. Baxter continued rummaging through his brother's clothes.

"I felt around Noel's neck and there was nothing there. I couldn't believe it. I was sure that we'd lost it. Then I saw his jacket from the night before on the floor and checked the pockets. There it was – my priceless Olympic medal, the symbol of all my hard work – soaked in beer and rammed into my little brother's pocket. The BOA looked relieved, I felt hungover as hell and we left for Salt Lake."

At the press conference Baxter found the amassed journalists better prepared, after some hurried research, than they had been the day before. They had all been caught off-guard by his success. They probed the Scotsman, looking for an angle for the next day's sports pages: Was it true he used to be a shinty player? Could he have been a professional ice hockey player? Why had he sprayed the Scottish Saltire flag into his hair? How had it felt to be asked to remove it by the BOA who'd said it could be perceived as a political statement? (Baxter's hair was completely blue as a result, having hastily filled in the white stripes.)

Alain Baxter with his 'Saltaire' hair cut

That night Baxter moved to the Olympic village for the first time. He had planned to fly to Canada after the Games to do some races but the BOA had realised he was front page news and suggested a change of plan. Baxter still hadn't seen a British newspaper and had no inkling that at home he'd become a household name overnight. Once the decision to return to the UK was made he was desperate to get back, but it was easier said than done.

"I really wanted to get back to Aviemore and see all my family and friends but I couldn't get a flight for two days. It was a very lonely time. The first night in the Olympic village I didn't go out because I was feeling so dreadful. I missed the closing ceremony. The next day the rest of the team flew to Canada. Then it was just me and Fiona. I did lots of telephone interviews and received lots of calls from sponsors. Jaguar even called up to offer me a car. I realised then that what I'd achieved was pretty big. It meant more than just being on a podium at a ski race. It was the Olympics. But I gave our team sponsor, Peugeot, the benefit of the doubt. I really, really fancied a Jag but I told Peugeot that if they gave the team another car I'd refuse it. They agreed, offering a new team car of my choice. It felt like the right thing to do. Peugeot had been good to the team and deserved a bit of loyalty.

"Later that day the BSSF office faxed over all the newspaper cuttings from the Games. That's when I truly realised what I'd achieved. I had tears in my eyes as I sat alone, thousands of miles from home, looking through hundreds of pages of press cuttings. There were pictures of my grandparents in one newspaper, my dad in another, and my mum and aunt too. It really hit home. I couldn't believe what I was seeing. It was so surreal to see my family and read what they were saying about me when I hadn't seen them myself."

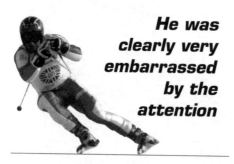

He was clearly very embarrassed by the attention

Baxter and McNeilly flew back to Edinburgh the following day, Baxter being the only British medallist to fly back economy class. McNeilly, Alain's constant companion for the Olympic rollercoaster ride of the past few days, remembers the flight home clearly.

"There was loads of fuss over Alain because his medal was setting off metal detectors everywhere. Everyone wanted an autograph and it was interesting to see how he was going to adapt to the new-found fame, knowing that he wasn't really comfortable with that side of things at all. I crashed out as soon as we got on the plane and they must have served coffee because when I woke up Alain looked over and said, 'Your coffee's cold but I saved a cookie for you.' I thought – you're not going to be changed by this at all. On the flight up from London the captain asked to see Alain's medal. He was clearly very embarrassed by the attention but had nowhere to hide."

If Baxter was uncomfortable with the attention of a handful of fellow passengers nothing would prepare him for the scene which awaited him at Edinburgh Airport. Stumbling off the plane, jet-lagged, exhausted, dehydrated and disoriented, Baxter was greeted by a cacophony of camera shutters clicking, bagpipes wailing, children screaming, and fans cheering. Yet another press conference beckoned, but more than anything Baxter wanted to be reunited with his mother to share the last leg of his journey home. Baxter would have to prepare himself for an even more astonishing homecoming in Aviemore. Unbeknown to him, the whole village was gathering to welcome home the local hero. The village butcher had already been doing a roaring trade in Baxter Burgers and the Cairngorm Hotel was serving up Baxter Bronze cocktails to the seemingly endless stream of journalists and photographers.

Despite having not slept for 24 hours, Baxter and his mother made two unscheduled stops on the three hour drive north. Baxter's mother brimmed with pride all the way. They stopped at Craigclowan Preparatory School in Perthshire where his cousin, Ross, was a former pupil. Though weary, Baxter was happy to officially open its new dry ski slope and show everyone his medal. Baxter stopped at Newtonmore School too and over twenty hours after leaving Salt Lake, he finally arrived home. After a swift shower and change (into non-Team GB clothing) Baxter was back out of the door quicker than he'd completed the Slalom course in Deer Valley. *The Daily Record* had laid on a tartan open-top bus to transport him and his family through the village to The Cairngorm Hotel, where a 'modest' homecoming party for family and close friends had been planned in his honour. Baxter thought the bus an extravagant gesture as he still had no inkling of the welcome he'd get at the hotel. It had sounded low key and just what he had hoped for after the madness of Edinburgh.

THE HERO RETURNS

"I met my family in a pub at the edge of the village. That was the first time I'd seen my grandparents. They were so happy and proud. Then we got on the bus and drove up the village. As we got nearer to the hotel the streets became busier and busier and everyone started shouting and screaming. I couldn't believe my eyes. There was loads of press there too. It was so overwhelming, the amount of people there and the organisation. They'd had virtually no time to arrange anything but there was live music, banners, food stalls and all the bikers I knew from the valley riding in front of the bus as we drove through the village."

2,000 people had turned out to welcome their favourite son home. It is a night which has entered local folklore and one that Baxter's father, Ian, will never forget.

"Everyone from the village and the area came out to welcome Alain home that night. The streets were lined, there was a sea of people outside The Cairngorm Hotel. It was unbelievable. People in the village have followed Alain's career from day one so they knew how hard he'd worked for his medal. Maybe that's what prompted their response. You could see that Alain was touched by it. He never expected it at all."

The open top bus would do a tour of the village before coming to rest at The Cairngorm Hotel where Baxter and his family struggled to make it through the crowd. Baxter's 76 year-old grandfather, Chic, was in the thick of things with his grandson.

"When we got off the bus the local kids pushed us out of the way to get to Alain. They were desperate to see the medal and get autographs. One boy had his leg in a full plaster, like Alain had when he was a young boy, but he was at the front with the rest of them, getting jostled around. Alain made a beeline straight for him."

It wasn't just the village children who were swamping Baxter. His mother, Sue, has another memory of the night which sticks out in her mind.

"Lots of local girls where getting Alain to sign his name across their chests. I gestured toward my own chest and he said, 'No family please.' The next girl had, let's say, the fuller figure, and Alain knew her husband. He wrote, 'Best wishes from Alain Baxter' on one side of her chest and, 'Sorry Steve!', on the other."

Baxter eventually worked his way through the crowd to a stage which had been hastily erected just hours before. He stood there as people applauded and cheered for a moment before taking an uncertain step forward to the microphone. He remembers it as it if was yesterday.

"I took the microphone and didn't know what to say. I was overwhelmed. I wasn't in front of a TV camera or a foreign crowd, it was live in front of the people that knew me best. All I said was, 'Thanks for coming. I'm not one for big speeches so party on!' That was the most emotional thing – being home at last. It was so full-on. Everywhere I went I was swamped by people wanting to congratulate me. My medal seemed to mean a lot to the people there. Maybe it was because I was someone they knew. I knew most of the people there, even if it was just to say hello to in the supermarket. There were people there I'd gone to school with, their parents were there, grandparents too. That's the type of place Aviemore is. It was a great homecoming. I couldn't have asked for more and I couldn't have been more touched by the response. It was one of the best days of my life."

When Baxter finally put his head on the pillow in the early hours of the morning he fell asleep in an instant. It had been an incredible couple of days. When he did dream he dreamt of his final run, of effortlessly passing gate after gate before crossing the line. He never dreamt of the ceremony and, far from coveting the medal, Baxter hadn't even noticed that he'd left the party without it. Baxter's rare Bronze medal was safely round the neck of his father. A father who'd never been so proud as when he saw his son up on that podium. A father who had to pinch himself to believe that he'd had two sons in the Olympic final. And Baxter slept on, sleeping the sleep of the righteous, safe in the knowledge that he would always have that medal to remind him of the events of the last few days. Sometime much later Aviemore fell quiet as the party subsided. There wasn't a sound to be heard in the remote village. All was well. But as Baxter innocently slumbered, dead to the world, events were unfolding in a laboratory halfway around the world which would shatter his dream forever.

> CHAPTER 2   **A FAMILY STORY**

A FLEDGLING SKI SCENE
QUICK OFF THE MARK
A COMPETITIVE STREAK
AN INTRODUCTION TO RACING
THE FINANCIAL BURDEN
LEAVING SCHOOL AT LAST

2   A FAMILY STORY

The Alain Baxter story does not start on December 26, 1973, when he was born prematurely in an Edinburgh hospital. Neither does it start on February 23, 2002, when he became Britain's first ever Olympic skiing medallist. It begins long before. Baxter's story is as much about the dynamic family he was born into, and his phenomenal success is linked intrinsically to the history of the small ski resort in the Highlands that he still calls home. The village of Aviemore, 35 miles south of Inverness in the heart of the Spey Valley, had been a magnet for tourists since Victorian times when the mainline railway was extended from Perth. But it was only in the 1950s that skiers began to cast wanton looks upon the snowy peaks of the Cairngorm Mountain range. The snow had always been there, of that there is no doubt, but at that time no ski lifts or infrastructure of any type existed. There wasn't even a road as far as the mountains.

But as Baxter would become accustomed to overcoming the obstacles checking his progress up the ranks of 6,000 registered international skiers, so too did his grandparents, Chic and Mae Baxter, to the challenge of skiing the uncharted slopes of Cairngorm. Baxter's grandparents were outdoor sports enthusiasts par excellence. If they weren't sailing, they'd be cycling. If they weren't ice skating, or playing ice hockey, they'd be skiing. They had even moved briefly from their native Dundee to Canada in pursuit of a better lifestyle but found that they could do more in Scotland and, crucially, had more friends there too.

"We were among the first people to ski in Aviemore," recalls Chic Baxter, who was one of the pioneers of the Highland ski scene in the 1950s. "We called ourselves 'The Walkers'. In winter we'd drive up with our two children, Ian (Alain's dad) and Lorna (Lesley McKenna's mother), and hike from the hayfield at Loch Morlich three miles to the top of Cairngorm carrying four pairs of skis and a rucksack. It was hard-going but we didn't force the kids to come. Mind you, the alternative was to stay with their granny all weekend.

"We'd carry our skies up on Saturday. Leave them up there overnight, stuck in the snow, and then hike back up on Sunday, find them and ski again. There was no lift at all for many years and the first lift of any sort was a rope line hooked up to a tractor that we'd move over to the back of the mountain in the summer so we could ski on any snow that remained. I got some funny looks from my neighbours in Dundee, tying skis on top of the car in the middle of August but if there was snow there, why not ski on it?"

A FLEDGLING SKI SCENE

But a sea change was about to occur in the sport that would give Aviemore its biggest facelift since it was put on the rail map in 1892. There had been a lobby to install a ski lift at Cairngorm since the first people had skied there in the post-war period. Throughout the 1950s a handful of Norwegians and Austrians had taken notice of Aviemore's abundance of snow and a fledgling ski scene started to take shape. But it was only in 1961, when Aviemore's first ski lift was installed, that skiing in Scotland suddenly became accessible and affordable to all. Bitten by the bug, and able to take advantage of improved access, Alain Baxter's father, Ian, soon became an accomplished skier. After making a name for himself on the Scottish scene with Dundee Ski Club, the apprentice fitter was given a £50 grant to travel to Val d'Isere to train with the British ski team.

We were among the first to ski in Aviemore

"It was like day and night compared to my usual life. The British team had this deserved reputation for being populated by the upper class. And it was mostly true. The guys I skied with were all army officers, such as Jeremy and Charles Palmer-Tomkinson, the uncle and father of IT girl Tara Palmer-Tomkinson. They, along with their father and elder brother, had all been British ski champions. It was almost unheard of for a working class boy like myself to be on the team."

Though skiing still hasn't shaken off the reputation of being a pastime of the privileged, it couldn't have been further from the truth in Aviemore. If you lived there in the 1960s and didn't ski, you were the exception to the rule. There were no pretensions, it was even an integral part of the curriculum at nearby Kingussie High School. But while the perception of skiing being the preserve of the privileged was slowly becoming outmoded, what was also true was that to make a career out of ski racing as a Brit you would have had to be born both with a supreme talent and to a family who found it *de riguer* to 'winter' in the Alps.

Despite these financial obstacles – obstacles which would still be in place when his eldest son would try and make a career out of skiing – Ian Baxter did enjoy great success as an amateur racer. He was Scottish ski champion in 1969 and became an established member of the British team. But the pragmatics of the time meant that if Ian Baxter was ever going to make a living out of the sport it was going to be through coaching. After meeting future wife Sue Field in the mid-1960s, Ian took a job at Hill End dry ski slope in her native Edinburgh. But the call of real snow was too much for them and within a year they had upped sticks and moved to Aviemore, where Sue got more involved in the race scene.

Ian had been introduced to Sue by his Scottish team-mate Kenny Dickson, who also went to live in Aviemore. The two friends soon landed jobs as some of the youngest ski instructors on the mountain as a boom in the sport drove demand for lessons. Sue too, trained as an instructor and soon the couple were making a modest living out of the sport they loved. But the pioneering spirit instilled in the couple by Chic and Mae Baxter – a mindset that would filter

By 1972 the Aviemore ski scene was in full swing

down to the next generation of the Baxter clan – was still there. When news of an unofficial Winter Commonwealth Games in St Moritz reached Aviemore the pull proved too powerful for the couple. Ian Baxter had all but retired from international racing by this time due to financial constraints but they put together a Scottish team, piled into a Ford Transit van and headed to the Alps. Ian and Sue would even share skis at the event. The DIY nature of the trip would later form the template for son Alain when he embarked on his own racing career.

By 1972 the Aviemore ski scene was in full swing. Millions had been spent turning the sleepy village into a winter holiday resort. Ski instructors from all over the Alps had boarded the gravy train to cash in on the boom and the village felt more like an Alpine resort than a Highland hamlet. The Stakis Hotel in the shadow of Cairngorm employed fifteen Swiss and three British instructors alone. There was an abundance of snow, season after season, and the local Ski Instructor's Championship was like a who's who of international skiing. Such was the talent amongst the instructors that it gave Ian Baxter an outlet to continue an international racing career cut short. Against all odds the mountain had come to Mohammed. Into this skiing Shangri-la was to be born a young child called Alain. If there was ever a family for a future world-class skier to be born into, if there were ever a place and a time for that skier to be born in Britain, this was it.

QUICK OFF THE MARK

Sue Baxter gave birth to her and Ian's first and only child together on Boxing Day, 1973, two weeks prematurely, whilst she was in Edinburgh visiting her parents over Christmas. Baxter's reputation for being quick out of the starting gate would later cause the family to reflect whether this had been an early sign of the strong will of an impatient baby.

It is a common misconception that Alain Baxter was named after French World Cup Slalom champion, Alain Penz, who Ian Baxter had once raced against in Aviemore. If true, what Alain Baxter would grow up to achieve would make that an apt and ironic choice, perhaps only surpassed in sport by former tennis world number 1, Martina Hingis, who was herself named after former tennis world number 1, Martina Navratilova. But though the exotic spelling of his name was influenced by the French skier, the true origin of his name is a secret known only by Ian Baxter.

"I remember reading *Kidnapped* by Robert Louis-Stevenson and there was a character called Alan Breck-Stewart. He was the hero of the book, a rebellious Highlander who had been a supporter of Bonnie Prince Charlie and had survived Culloden. I'd always had the name in mind for our son. This was long before I'd heard of Alain Penz. But then I'd started to see the French spelling and I thought it was a bit different. So our son was named Alain Rory Baxter."

It didn't take Baxter long to get his first taste of winter sports. As a baby growing up in a house full of skiing equipment, by his first birthday he had already learnt to fix a ski boot into a binding and stand unaided in the boots, which dwarfed him. Unfortunately, the connubial bliss he was born into would not last for long. In the summer of 1975 Sue Baxter moved out of the marital home taking her son with her.

"When Alain and I moved out, living in a caravan was the only option for us. I couldn't afford anything else. The first caravan didn't even have running water or electricity. We had to get water out of a stream and there was an outdoor toilet which we had to empty every now and then. That was the first summer. By winter I realised that there was no way we'd survive in those conditions – Alain was still an infant – so we moved to a slightly bigger caravan which had electricity and running water. It was still pretty basic but we had some good years there together."

Christmas 1974

Baxter's father continued to play a big part in his life, despite the separation, and was never far away. With both parents so heavily involved in skiing it was inevitable that it wouldn't take long for him to take to the slopes. Though Baxter has little recollection of it – "I don't even remember actually learning to ski. I've always known," – fortunately his mother has a clearer picture.

"I was dating Kenny Dickson by this stage who was separated from his wife and had a son and daughter of his own. We weren't yet married but were both working ski instructors when Alain was growing up. Quite often the option to leave him, Natasha and Aubrey at home wasn't there. We didn't have babysitters so we had to take them up the hill.

"Aubrey was six and Natasha was four, so they were already skiing. Having seen this, Alain was desperate to go. The first day he went up – Alain would have been almost three – he had on these plastic Mothercare skis, which clipped onto his shoes. It was his first time on the snow and I had him between my legs to stop him falling or running away down the hill. He soon got the hang of it. Later that morning Aubrey skied past us on his own and Alain spotted him out of the corner of his eye. Before I knew it he had broken free of me and tore off down the hill after him. That was it, after that he was on his own."

Out on the slopes at Aviemore 1979

Ian Baxter remembers skiing with Alain around the same time.

"Alain started skiing when he was two. It was a matter of fact that he would ski. All the children in Aviemore were the same. As soon as they could balance on skis they were off. We didn't really teach Alain, he just copied myself, Sue and Kenny."

It was soon clear that the young Alain Baxter had inherited all his parents' and grandparents' natural athleticism and verve for life. By the age of five, though still small for his age, he was well-built and athletic. He had good balance and impressive coordination for one so young, as future stepfather, Kenny Dickson, recalls.

"Alain could turn his hand to most sports. He was always up to something when he was young. He wasn't the sort to sit around and colour-in a picture. Whatever he did he was always looking to get better at it. We got him a BMX bike and within weeks he'd be riding down the street on one wheel. He had a skateboard and learnt to ride it on his hands at a very young age. The same went for skiing."

It wasn't all plain sailing where Baxter's taste for adventure was concerned. Father, Ian, remembers one occasion in March 1979 when the youngster came unstuck.

"When Alain was five he fell skiing and broke his leg. It was at Easter, in wet, soggy snow. He had to get a full-length plaster because he was so young. He'd had it on for six weeks when we went to Raigmore Hospital to get the cast off. In the doctor's surgery the X-Ray of his leg was up on the screen. I saw straight away that where he'd broken the leg the bones didn't meet up. There was a big gap. I never thought Alain would notice so I kept quiet and

Alain in the plaster cast

planned to ask the Doctor later. But Alain noticed immediately and said, 'It's not fixed dad. It hasn't healed.' The doctor explained that they had to keep the bones apart so they could grow together so he wouldn't have one leg shorter than the other. Alain didn't ask about it again.

"When the plaster came off he might as well have had one leg shorter than the other. He couldn't walk because there was no muscle in the leg. Alain had got so used to leaning on the plaster, he'd been playing football with it on, he was up and down the chute at the playpark, that when it came off he was walking like Quasimodo. The recovery was quick though. And then as soon as it snowed he was up skiing straight away. He had no fear."

By the winter of 1979 Sue Baxter realised that three years in a caravan with a young child was enough and she and Alain moved in with Kenny Dickson and his son Aubrey at 9 Railway Terrace. Aubrey and Alain would share a tiny bedroom with space only for two bunks but it was a novelty for the boy who had only known life in a caravan with his mum and he never complained once. Soon the couple would buy the house next-door and knock through the wall to create number 9 1/2 Railway Terrace.

At the age of 7, Baxter was already skiing alone at Cairngorm when conditions allowed. The 'Hats, Gloves, Goggles, Skis, Boots, Sticks and Pass' checklist became a mantra on Railway Terrace. There were three generations of Baxters regularly skiing at Cairngorm by this time, Baxter's grandparents, Chic and Mae having moved up from Dundee. Their daughter Lorna had also moved up and married local ski racer, Willie McKenna. Their daughters, Lesley and Nancy, were like sisters to Baxter. And so a skiing dynasty was born. Chic Baxter recalls one incident on Cairngorm that still amuses Baxter's grandparents to this day.

"When Alain was seven he skied past us with some friends. We were in the queue for the lift and thought he'd want nothing to do with us but he yelled over, 'Can I ski with you granny?' You won't hear that said on many ski slopes."

A COMPETITIVE STREAK

Away from the parental glare Baxter was becoming an extremely accomplished skier for his age and developing a competitive edge that would set him apart from his peers within only a few years. After having not skied with him for just a couple of weeks Baxter's mother was surprised to see how far he'd come in such a short time.

"One day I noticed that Alain had become quite competitive when he was skiing. It was really windy that day so Alain had to ski with me and Kenny because he was still so young and small. It was too windy at the top for him so I took him between my legs on the t-bar. En-route to the top we'd drop Alain off halfway and tell him we'd ski down from the top and catch him up."

"The first time we did this we caught up with him three-quarters of the way down the piste, as we'd intended. The next time we dumped him off in the same place and when we caught up with him he was a lot nearer the bottom than the time before. The next time he was even further down and the next time we did it he was leaning on his skis at the bottom saying, 'What kept you?' After that we just took him to the top with us."

For all his progress on skis, Baxter's performance at the local primary school left a lot to be desired. He had a reputation for being a fidget, for having a short concentration span and his reading and writing were so bad that teachers thought he was dyslexic. He was even offered remedial help one term but Baxter didn't have learning difficulties. Already at a young age, he knew academia would not be a big part of his life and he spent his days counting down the minutes until the school bell rang and he could get outside to play.

Baxter's homelife was extremely settled by the turn of the decade. His mother and father had both remarried and he would soon have a half-brother, Noel, and sister, Lucie, from Ian Baxter's second marriage. He had his own bedroom by this time too, after his mother and stepfather had knocked the two houses on Railway Terrace together. Not that it meant that the house was any less cramped. The Dicksons had gained a reputation for almost limitless hospitality, as Baxter's mother recalls:

"Aviemore was very cosmopolitan and relaxed back then. We never locked our door because that's the type of place Aviemore is, and often we'd come down on a Saturday morning and half of Kendal, where Europa Sport and the Kastle Ski people were based, would be there. We knew them through the ski schools and they'd have driven up in the night to get on the snow early. There'd be people sleeping in beds, on sofas, on the floor, under the dining table. In the morning I'd cook a massive fry-up and we'd all go up the hill skiing together. It got to the stage where I'd look out of the window in the morning before going downstairs and if I saw four Europa Sport cars I would go straight out and buy provisions for breakfast. It was a great atmosphere for Alain to grow up in though, especially after the years in the caravan."

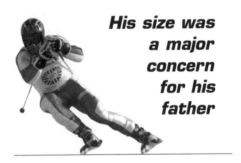

His size was a major concern for his father

From learning with his parents, to skiing every Wednesday afternoon with his school, it didn't take Baxter long to progress to the Cairngorm Ski Club (CSC), which conducted ski training and arranged races throughout the winter. It was more about having fun than actual training but Baxter threw himself into it, catching the attention of one or two of the coaches in the process. His size was a major concern for father, Ian, however.

"He was really tiny then, the smallest in his class. He was always really athletic but he was so small. It's amazing he's actually grown to the size he is now. You would never have thought it back then."

Despite his size, Baxter was also following in the footsteps of his father and grandfather in developing a love of ice hockey. Boasting a professional team, The Aviemore Blackhawks, regular training sessions and games were held at the village ice rink. He'd be the smallest boy on the ice but got a reputation for being fast and skilful. For the first time Baxter was faced with a conundrum when Saturdays came around during the winter: skiing or ice hockey? As Baxter explains, it could have been a conundrum if he'd had any say in the matter.

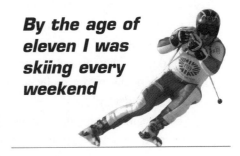

By the age of eleven I was skiing every weekend

"By the age of eleven I was skiing every weekend so mum bought me a season ticket. I was over the moon. But then the ice hockey season started and I wanted to go and play on a Saturday. But she would say, 'No, you're going skiing. I didn't spend all that money for nothing. You've got a season ticket so you're going up'. So that was that. Mum and Kenny weren't that flush so I had to go along with it."

AN INTRODUCTION TO RACING

The conflict between ice hockey and skiing would be short-lived. Unbeknown to Baxter, a chance invitation to go skiing in the Alps would give him his first taste of top level racing and make his mind up for good. It was Baxter's first foreign trip and one he would never forget.

"Fraser and Bridget Clyde invited me to go to Switzerland with them for three weeks over Christmas. They'd been racers before and knew my parents. Their kids were Robbie and Josie. Robbie was 11 too, and a good friend of mine though he went to a private school nearby. He was also the best skier in our age group.

"We went to their chalet in Les Diabrelets. We did lots of skiing but got up to lots of mischief as well. We used to sledge at nightime on the road between Les Diabrelets and Villar. Bridget would go behind us in the car and shine the lights and we would be battering down in front on these really old fashioned wooden sledges, trying to dig our heels in to turn.

"After a couple of weeks Fraser said he was going to take us to Austria for some races. He entered us in the British Junior Championships, which was a bit daunting. I didn't really know what I was doing. I could ski anywhere, my standard of skiing was high, but when it came to racing I didn't have a bloody clue, I'd never been properly coached. But I loved the buzz of competing and that's where the racing really started for me. When I came back I started racing straightaway."

Baxter's mother has her own recollection of the epiphany-causing holiday and admits she was reluctant to encourage her son to get into racing.

"Because Robbie was racing a lot overseas even then, Bridget and Fraser Clyde had been saying to us for ages, 'Come on, you've got to get Alain racing too.' But we'd said, 'No way'. It was just far too expensive for us and we didn't want him to be disappointed further down the line. When he went on holiday to Switzerland with the Clydes we didn't know that they were going to go racing. So unbeknown to us Fraser had been training Alain and they took him off to the British Junior Championships. He came tenth, after just one week's Slalom training, which we had to admit was incredible."

Though Baxter's early success and exposure to racing would cement his interest in the sport, it fell to stepfather Kenny to explain the harsh realities to the ambitious youngster.

"We didn't say outright that he couldn't do it but we didn't really want Alain to go the racing route. I remember the look on his face when I said, 'Alain, you'll be so frustrated. We won't have the money to do it properly and you'll end up being very disappointed.' His heart sank but what I told him was true and it happened exactly as I'd said it would. There were loads of times we couldn't afford equipment or training camps and had to find sponsorship for him. What we never realised, however, was that he would be quite so determined."

Though all he wanted to do was grow up to be an international Slalom racer, Baxter was pragmatic. He knew, after seeing their children's clothing business collapse, that his mother and Kenny couldn't fund his dream. He'd remembered being the last person in the Cairngorm Ski Club to get a club jacket and salopettes, and wearing them until they fell off him. He could see that the people he'd race against were better off, attending private schools and with parents with chalets in the Alps. This was nothing new to him. But he also saw a burgeoning domestic race scene on his doorstep.

"When I came back from Austria I started skiing in the Scottish Junior Series races. I was travelling to every race in the country – The West of Scotland at Glencoe, The East of Scotland at Glenshee and the North of Scotland at Cairngorm, they were the three big circuits. Back then the Scottish scene was massive. Cairngorm Ski Club had about 100 people in it alone. Then there was the Scottish Ski Club which was even bigger with people from Edinburgh and Glasgow, then Bearsden Ski Club, and Dolphin Ski Club.

"There were four or five clubs training on Cairngorm. They used to give out priority bibs for the ski lift to people training but the priority queue was bigger than the normal queue. I'd race or train every weekend with CSC, every Christmas break, every Easter break, every half-term and return to Fulpmes in Austria for the British Junior Championships each season if we could scrape together the money. Having experienced it once I wanted to go again and again until I won it."

And so Baxter would spend every winter until his early teens, improving with every season. At this exciting time in Baxter's development he was fortunate to be surrounded on the team by friends he'd known all his life. A group of extremely talented young skiers emerged from Cairngorm including Baxter, McKenna, Andrew Freshwater, Peter Ferguson, and Richie Hart. Baxter was already developing a talent for the technical skiing disciplines: Slalom, Giant Slalom (SG) and Super G, despite, by his own admission, being:

"A tiny little dude, banging into all the gates, who was so small that they were almost stopping me every time I hit them."

By 13 Baxter was well-established on the Scottish race scene and was about to meet a coach who would inspire and instil in him a real belief in his potential. Colin Grant, who had trained under Baxter's mother, had gone on to race at international level. But, like so many racers, Grant's career was cut short by injury. Returning to his home in Granton-on-Spey, near Aviemore, Grant began taking race training at CSC. His recent exposure to international racing shone through in his coaching and had an immediate effect on Baxter.

"In the early days Colin's coaching was really important for me. I'd say he was one of the biggest influences on my career. He had so much wisdom because he'd been there and done it. When Colin was coaching me that's when I really realised that I wanted to make a career out of racing. Colin was massively supportive. When I was fourteen he said that I'd definitely go to the Olympics in Lillehammer in 1994. It was a huge confidence boost and he was later nearly proven right. I could have gone but I peaked too late that season and the selectors thought I was too young."

THE FINANCIAL BURDEN

By 14 Baxter had broken into the Scottish Junior Ski Team and was gaining ever-more exposure to international racing and training camps. But with that came the financial burden that Baxter's parents had been dreading. Having recently seen a business fail, Sue and Kenny Dickson's only income was from instructing during the winter. Even they would admit that they did it more for the lifestyle than the meagre income. Kenny did some occasional marketing for ski manufacturers, though the greatest benefit to come out of that was free or subsidised skis for Baxter at a time when no other manufacturer would dare sponsor an unproven 14-year-old. Determined not to miss out on the valuable overseas training camps and races a still shy Baxter, a figure totally at odds with the one who'd ski so aggressively and play ice hockey with such skill and passion, would join forces with his mother to appeal for potential sponsors for the trips. In a process that would become second nature, Baxter would sit with his mother and dictate his hopes and dreams for a glittering ski career for the benefit of would-be sponsors, if only he could attend the next camp...

Even then Baxter had his sights set high and would start each letter, "It has always been my ambition to ski in the Olympics for Great Britain." Baxter's mother, who had spent countless hours trying to get her son to do his homework in the past, was surprised at how he took to the task.

"I'd sit with Alain and we'd put together a portfolio to send out to try and raise a bit of money. It was the type of thing that he hated but he soon

realised that it was the only way he was going to be able to go on any trip. We just didn't have the money. We'd get sent a breakdown of how much the camps were going to cost. Every time we got one we thought, 'Here we go again!' and I'd be on the phone to my sister who'd pass it on to her husband who would help Alain out if we couldn't raise the money elsewhere."

But all the hard work on and off the piste was paying off. Baxter was posting ever-improving results, often against older skiers. At this stage Baxter was still skiing across all disciplines. In the Giant Slalom (GS), Baxter finished 21st in the 1986 Scottish Junior Championships. One year later he finished 6th and in 1988 he was 5th. A 24th place finish in the GS at the British Junior Championships in 1987 was improved to an 8th place one year later. In short, Baxter was an improving skier, but he was still not the best in his age group. Yet something set Baxter apart from his peers. Despite sharing the reservations of Sue and Kenny Dickson about Alain's proposed career in ski racing, Ian Baxter had seen something in his son that he'd seen in the top racers of his day.

"I knew all along that he had the talent to race at the top level. But more than that he had a determination. I knew how tough it would be to do it properly, how long it would take, how hard he would have to work. I would have said that the obstacles in his way were insurmountable. The funding alone could have stopped him. At that time no-one had done it, had come through from the British scene to achieve anything. I was involved with training a lot of kids before Alain and I knew that someone was going to have to commit to skiing right into their thirties if we were going to see success in Britain. Alain was the first one who looked at it as a full-time career. He knew he had to work his way up the Scottish scene, then British Team, then the low-ranking senior events, the Citaden, FIS, Europa Cup and Nor-Am Cup tours, and eventually, if he had the talent, to break into the World Cup, World Championship and Olympic scene."

Vindication for all Baxter's hard work came in 1987 when he was first selected to join the British Junior Team. It was a major breakthrough for the young skier, proof that his dedication and persistence were starting to pay off. But he knew that he wasn't at the end of the journey. It had just begun. Despite finishing just 29th and 49th in consecutive international GS races in Abetone and Saas-Fee, and a creditable 21st in the Slalom, Baxter's cousin Lesley, who was also on the team, began to see her cousin in a new light.

"When Alain first went to an International Children's Race, he didn't look at the other skiers and go, 'They're from the Alps and I'm only from Scotland. I'm never going to be able to beat them.' He never blew it out of proportion or was there for the wrong reasons. He was just there doing a job, and he knew what that job was, and he'd known since he first saw international racing. He knew immediately what it was going to take to be on a level with everyone else, whether they were from the Alps, Canada or Scotland. That's what set him apart.

"To get to the top in any sport you have to know what the level is at the top before you can reach it, to know what the people who are best at the sport do, how they think, how they feel, how they live, what matters to them. Alain did that from a very young age. Alain never felt threatened by the Alpine nations because skiing had always been such a big part of our lives. As kids we sat and watched our grandad's Super 8 films of the Alps, that was normal to us. Our grandparents would say to us, 'You're definitely going to be a Slalom/Downhill racer.' It didn't seem odd to Alain that he could do that. He had comments like this ingrained into his psyche and it showed when he came up against better foreign skiers. He was one of them, not an outsider like so many other British skiers had been."

What shines through from Baxter's early years as a Junior international racer was how unintimidated he was by the enormity of the challenge. It is said that the risk-taking, and risk-accepting ethos instilled into him at a young age by his grandparents made him fit in better with his Alpine opponents than fellow members of his team. Baxter had been living an Alpine lifestyle in the Highlands all his life. He'd been surrounded by the foreign instructors his parents knew and he'd seen that it was possible to make a career out of the sport. It was in his blood. Yet when Baxter made the giant leap out of the domestic race scene onto the international level in his mid-teens he never felt like he'd made it. He'd known how his father had come this far only to be thwarted. So while many of Baxter's British team-mates arrogantly puffed up their chests with pride and resigned themselves to defeat by their foreign rivals, Baxter was finishing down the rankings too but, far from treating his victors with undeserved contempt or unnecessary reverence, he was introducing himself to them. He was picking out the boy who had won the race and wondering, 'What's he like? Where does he live? How does he train? What skis is he using? Where can I get a pair?

He'd seen it was possible to make a career out of the sport

LEAVING SCHOOL AT LAST

For all his progress in the ski world, some things never changed with Baxter. He'd been attending Kingussie High School since 1985 with little distinction. Teachers there reported the same problems he'd had at primary school – he'd spend lessons dreaming of being out cycling, playing shinty, ice hockey, or skiing. But they tolerated Baxter because alongside McKenna, Ferguson and Freshwater he was on the Scottish Ski Team and was regularly winning accolades for the school. But Baxter had decided long before that school just didn't agree with him.

"I was counting down the days in school from when I was 14. People were taking more notice of me now on the ski circuit. I'd progressed to the British Junior Team. Skiing was what I wanted to do. I had no doubt. The school had always known that this would be the case and to be fair to them they never said I was wasting my time. They knew I was never going to end up in an office."

Once Baxter had made clear his intention to leave, there was no holding him back. Well, as it turned out, there was. Despite nearing the end of his 4th year at the school Baxter was not yet 16 – the minimum leaving age. It fell to Baxter's mother to broker a compromise.

"Alain's 16th birthday wasn't until Boxing Day so the school wouldn't let him go until Christmas unless he was going into full-time education. Much to his displeasure, we got him a place on a short course at Inverness College and the school agreed to let him leave in the summer."

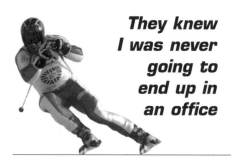

They knew I was never going to end up in an office

It wasn't Baxter's perfect choice but at least it got him one step closer to skiing full-time. He'd leave school in the summer at the same time as Ronald Ross, who went on to become the greatest shinty player to have played the game. The pair would start their course in September. It wasn't the only option open to Baxter as it turned out. As he prepared to begin college an old family friend made a proposal. Baxter's mother remembers how quickly it took home-loving Baxter, who was already daunted about the prospect of having to travel to Inverness every day, to reject the offer.

"Roger Morrison, one of our old friends from Europa Sport in Kendal, offered Alain the chance to train as a ski technician. I remember we were sitting in the kitchen and he said to me, 'I don't think I can do it mum.' I asked him why not. I thought it was a great opportunity for him. 'Because Kendal has got a Boots and Marks & Spencer. It's far too big for me.'"

For all his travels with skiing, Baxter had never really known day-to-day life outside the idyllic village. He'd gone to nursery, primary school and secondary school with the same people. He knew everyone in the village and within its boundaries he wanted for virtually nothing. But for all his contentedness with life in the shadow of Cairngorm, a burning ambition flickered inside the young Highlander which would challenge his parochialism. There had already been one snow-less winter in Aviemore and having achieved as much as he could ever achieve on the Scottish ski circuit Baxter knew that the day would come when he would have to up-sticks for the Alps and scrap it out on the adult race circuit alongside the other 5,999 registered international racers. That would be a whole new ball game for the ambitious teenager, not least because he would have to figure out how on earth he was going to fund his expensive dream.

Alain BAXTER

> CHAPTER 3   **TESTING TIMES**

A SHOCK TO THE SYSTEM
UNDER COVER OF DARKNESS
FINDING THE CAUSE
THE STORY LEAKS OUT
THE TIDE BEGINS TO TURN

3   **TESTING TIMES**

On the morning of February 28, 2002, Sue Dickson woke her son from a much-needed slumber. For the first few seconds as he rubbed the sleep out of his eyes and stretched his aching limbs, Baxter's mind was a blank canvas, but then there was a noticeable flicker in his eyes and a broad smile broke across his face. Sue Baxter smiled too: her son the Olympic medallist – who would have thought it?

Later that day Baxter visited family, retrieved his medal from his father and enjoyed a quiet night in with his mother. The two had a close bond, borne from the days when they'd roughed it in a caravan, and were never more at ease than when together. There'd been bad times but this was very much the best of times.

On the morning of Friday February 29, Baxter completed a gruelling training session. It was his intention to return and finish the season, culminating in the prestigious World Cup Finals in Altenmarkt. It was a real chance for him to break into the World top ten. Before that, Baxter wanted to honour a few long-standing obligations. One was to Aviemore Primary School, the school he had attended as a boy. Some of the teachers that had taught him were still there and later that morning he returned to show the current pupils the real version of the Olympic medal he'd drawn in art class as a boy.

"I was embarrassed when I visited the school because I forgot the medal. I sat down with the kids for a chat and one girl, the tiniest little thing, came up to me with a bunch of flowers and was hugging my leg. I felt like a right idiot because all they really wanted to see was the medal, so I told them I'd come back the next day and they all cheered."

While Baxter masked his embarrassment at his former school, Fiona McNeilly was about to receive a mysterious telephone call from the BOA.

"Sometime on Friday morning I got a call from Philip Pope. He said gravely, 'Fiona, it's very important that we know where you are this weekend. Simon Clegg (Chef de Mission of the BOA) needs you to be reachable all weekend.' It was all very cloak and dagger. I didn't have a clue what was going on. I told him I'd have my mobile switched on all weekend."

In the afternoon, Baxter arranged a couple of newspaper interviews for the following day and set about arranging something far more enjoyable – a night out with his best friends. It had been the night he'd looked forward to since winning the medal. Numerous text messages went back and forth between the friends and they arranged to meet at 7pm. Baxter then turned off his mobile phone to escape the barrage of calls from press and well-wishers alike. No sooner had he done so than the landline in his mother's house began to ring.

A SHOCK TO THE SYSTEM

"I was about to jump in the shower when the phone rang. It was Simon Clegg from the BOA. I thought he was just calling for a chat or to arrange another press conference, but he didn't seem in the mood for small talk and asked me if I was sitting down. He got straight to the point. He said, 'Alain, I've just received notification from the IOC that your urine sample from Salt Lake has tested positive for a banned substance.' I was stunned. I thought he might have been joking so I said, 'You're kidding, aren't you?' But he wasn't. My heart sank. I was speechless, numb. I said, 'How can that be? I don't understand.' I asked Simon what I'd tested positive for and the

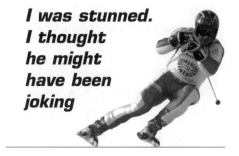

I was stunned. I thought he might have been joking

first thing he said was that there was a lot of it, whatever it was. He said, 'Alain, there's clear and then there's well over the limit. You were the latter.' 'But for what?' I asked. I had no idea what he was telling me. I just couldn't comprehend it."

Clegg explained that Baxter's sample was found to contain 500 nanograms per millilitre (later confirmed to be just 25 ng/ml) of Methamphetamine. Neither knew exactly what Methamphetamine was but they'd later learn that it is an illegal stimulant more commonly know as Crystal Meth or Speed.

Baxter's first thought was that Methamphetamine sounded very illegal and not something that could ever have been in his system. He was reeling.

"I think Simon was as confused as me. He asked me to get the wash-bag I'd taken to Salt Lake and we went through everything in it. I hadn't taken anything before my race that wasn't in the bag apart from meals at the athlete food hall and the house. Nothing in the bag seemed too untoward, though there was a Vicks Sinex product that my coach had bought for me. I'd only used it once, days before the race, then refused to use it again because it was stronger than the Vick's Inhaler product I usually used to unblock my nose. In any case, the team doctor had cleared it before I'd used it."

Clegg advised Baxter to leave Aviemore that evening and to travel to London. An official inquiry would follow in Lausanne which he'd be required to attend and the IOC was going to put out a statement saying that an unnamed British skier had failed a doping test. The story could break at any minute. Baxter initially refused to leave his home, telling Clegg that he was innocent and had nothing to hide. Clegg reiterated his advice, explaining that it was critical to test everything in his wash-bag at the BOA lab so they could establish how he had ingested a banned substance. It would be the first step on the road to clearing his name.

Baxter's mother had heard her son speaking in hushed tones on the telephone and sensed something wasn't right. When Baxter walked back into the room the first thing she noticed was that he was as white as a sheet.

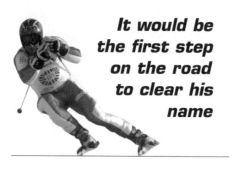

It would be the first step on the road to clear his name

"I don't think I've ever heard Alain swear before but when he got off the phone he said, 'Mum, I'm f**ked. I'm so f**ked. I don't know what's going on but my career is over.' I was shocked and when he explained everything I couldn't comprehend it. I didn't question him for a second because I knew how hard he'd worked to get on that podium. I tried to calm him down but he kept repeating himself: 'Mum, you have no idea how big this is going to be. This is the first time that a skier has tested positive for anything.'"

Baxter and his mother wracked their brains for anything that could have caused the positive test. They went through his wash-bag again but found nothing. Baxter occasionally chewed tobacco, a habit his mother despised, and she was sure that it would be to blame. But the tobacco had been cleared by the team doctor and he'd all but given up the habit. They were stumped and sat in silence. When the phone rang again they both jumped. They prayed it wasn't the press. Not now. But it was McNeilly. Clegg had called her just moments before delivering the devastating news to Baxter:

"Simon called me and said straight away, 'As team manager I have to inform you that one of our skiers has recorded a positive drugs test.' He asked me how I would react if he told me it was Alain? I said that I was absolutely stunned. I knew how clean he was. He wouldn't even take dietary supplements or drink coffee.

"I'm glad I responded like I did because my reaction, and Alain's, were important to Simon. He was under pressure to make a decision on whether the BOA should touch this or not. I think Alain's genuine shock told Simon what he needed to hear. I spoke to Alain straight after and the first thing he said was, 'What's going on Fiona?' He sounded lost."

McNeilly repeated Clegg's advice for Baxter to leave his mother's house as soon as possible and it was agreed that he would go early the next morning and travel to McNeilly's house in Edinburgh. At 6am the following morning Baxter hurriedly gathered some clothes. The last thing he packed was his Olympic medal. He paused briefly to look at it as he threw it into his suitcase. He'd worked so hard for the medal but more than the possibility of losing it, the realisation was dawning on Baxter that his career was probably over. Innocent or not, drugs scandals had a habit of never going away. In Lausanne the IOC would be well within its rights to take Baxter's medal back, disqualify him, and recommend a two-year ban from the sport. That was as good as a life sentence for his career.

UNDER COVER OF DARKNESS

Baxter left like a fugitive under cover of darkness and drove south with his mother on the deserted A9. The snow-capped Cairngorms loomed threateningly over the car and seemed to usher it out of the valley. At McNeilly's house the pair embraced. She'd witnessed Baxter's moment of glory and couldn't believe that it was all turning sour. The first thing she did was to shave Baxter's head. He still had blue hair and the remnants of the Saltire flag on his head, and was far too recognisable for McNeilly's liking. With husband, Gordon, banished to another room, told only that there was a slight problem with Baxter's medal, the Scot's appearance was transformed.

"When I told Alain that we'd have to shave his hair off he said, 'It's just getting to a length I like.' I ignored him. I didn't want people at every service station staring at him as we made our way to London. We had a few conversations about what could have caused the positive test. A lot of that centred on the Vick's Sinex, but nothing in his bag said it contained Methamphetamine. It was baffling.

"We drove to London in my Nissan Micra. I didn't want to go down in a team car in case we were recognised by anyone. In the car the conversation was surreal. Alain asked, 'So, who does the cooking at home?' then, 'This

Micra fairly zips along when it gets going doesn't it?,' then he'd come back to the realisation of the trouble he was in. I think he was still in shock."

If he hadn't felt like a fugitive before, Baxter certainly did now, speeding along into the great unknown, ignoring every call or message received on his phone. One call that he repeatedly rejected was from BSSF Performance Director, Graham Bell. Bell eventually called McNeilly's phone to ask if she knew where Baxter was. McNeilly reluctantly passed over the phone.

"Graham knew nothing about the failed test. He'd been looking through my contracts and said, 'Alain, I've got some great news, you've just won £20,000 in bonuses.' I didn't know what to say. I knew I'd never get to see the money: 'That's brilliant Graham, thanks'. Inside I was cursing my bad luck."

Baxter left like a fugitive under cover of darkness

McNeilly chatted briefly with Bell before telling him everything. Clegg had been implicit with his instructions and was especially against Bell knowing because of his contacts at the BBC. It was an explosive story and could have been a world exclusive for the broadcaster. But Bell was McNeilly's closest colleague and she trusted him.

"I was in turmoil and skirted round the issue but eventually said, 'I've got some really bad news. What is the worst thing you can imagine?' Graham had no patience. He said, 'I can imagine a lot of bad things. Just tell me what's wrong.' I could tell that he was referring to a tragedy we'd suffered when one of our team, Kirsteen McGibbon, had died skiing a few years before. It gave me a bit of much-needed perspective but at the time losing Alain's medal seemed like the end of the world."

In London McNeilly dropped Baxter off at the home of his ex-team-mate and friend, Jonny Moulder-Brown. Baxter would lie low at the Chelsea house until the results of the wash-bag tests were known. Later at Bell's house, McNeilly took a call from her husband. It would provide the first glimmer of hope in what had been twelve dark hours.

"Gordon called, though he wasn't supposed to know what had happened. I think he was as worried about my position at the Federation as he was about

Alain. He must have overheard us speaking about Vick's and Meth-amphetamine because he'd done some internet research and found some information about commercial pilots in the US who had been getting so called 'false positive' results for Methamphetamine in mandatory drugs tests, despite never having touched the drug. Further tests had shown that all the pilots who had specifically used the US version of a Vick's Inhaler, containing a separate and legal, but chemically identical, compound to Methamphetamine called Levmetamfetamine. I knew that Alain had both a Vick's Sinex and Vick's Inhaler but he'd told me that both of them had been given the all-clear by the team doctor, either in Salt Lake or long before. I couldn't remember if Alain's Vick's Inhaler was a European version or not, but it sounded like too much of a coincidence. I let Alain and the BOA know straight away."

FINDING THE CAUSE

The next day the BOA laboratory scrutinized the contents of Baxter's wash-bag. Every item was clear except one – the Vick's Inhaler. It contained L-metamfetamine, otherwise known as Levmetamfetamine, but not the illegal compound, Methamphetamine, that the IOC had claimed to have found. The BOA knew immediately that the harmless and legal ingredient had triggered the 'false' positive test for Methamphetamine in the IOC's rudimentary test. It was agonising but at last it seemed that Baxter and the BOA had something tangible to take to the IOC. Furthermore, it could

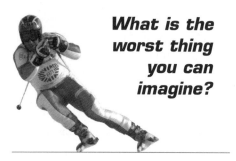

What is the worst thing you can imagine?

recommend a simple secondary test on Baxter's sample, known as Isomer Separation Analysis (ISA), which is widely used by other sporting federations and in workplace drug testing in the US to distinguish between Methamphetamine and its harmless cousin, Levmetamfetamine, in cases where initial tests have apparently flagged Methamphetamine. The test is 100 per cent conclusive, and well-documented, and it would be absolutely crucial to Baxter's defence that the IOC conduct it. It would prove for once and for all that the harmless medicinal compound in the inhaler had triggered Baxter's positive test.

The BOA was relieved to have isolated the cause of the false positive test, yet there was confusion as to how he'd come to ingest the substance. Team GB athletes were instructed to consult with the team doctor before taking anything. It didn't take the skier long to realise he'd made a costly error before the Games. Unhappy with, and ironically, wary of, the Vick's Sinex product that his coach had given him, Baxter had bought a US version of a Vick's Inhaler to replace it. As the product he'd used in Europe for ten years had virtually identical packaging and seemed for all intents and purposes to be the same product, he bought and used it without checking with the team doctor. He'd had the European version of the inhaler, which unbeknown to him had a different formula (not containing Levmetamfetamine), cleared on numerous occasions. It was a reckless but ultimately innocent act. A schoolboy error.

The BOA didn't doubt Baxter's version of events for a minute. BOA Legal Director, Sara Friend, recalls her first encounter with Baxter:

"As soon as we were introduced I could see that he genuinely didn't know what had caused the failed test. He had no idea. He comes across as someone who is so obviously honest. I couldn't see cheating in him at all. There was no attempt to hide anything from us. He was as desperate as us to get to the bottom of it so we had complete belief in him from very early on."

Given a few days the BOA would learn that Methamphetamine and Levmetamfetamine are recognised in science as completely separate and distinct substances (by almost every official body except the IOC). Despite having the same molecular formula they are optical isomers: Methamphetamine is to Levmetamfetamine what an object is to its reflection. The key distinction is that the two have very different pharmacological properties with only Methamphetamine boasting any significant stimulant properties, hence its illegality. Levmetamfetamine is completely legal, harmless and used exclusively in over-the-counter decongestants.

Once this became apparent it was something for Baxter to cling onto. A test existed which the IOC could do to determine that the 'Methamphetamine' found was in fact the harmless Levmetamfetamine. Surely it would be happy to conduct the test? Armed with this information,

Baxter, Clegg, McNeilly and Friend made a mad dash to Oxford on the Monday morning. They went to seek the counsel of revered QC, Michael Beloff, whom Clegg had recommended to Baxter.

As Baxter and Clegg charged ahead up the M40 in Clegg's high-powered Rover, McNeilly tried valiantly to keep up in her compact Nissan. Clegg explained to Baxter that Beloff is one of the top legal minds in Europe. He is also an experienced arbitrator with the Court of Arbitration for Sport (CAS), the most powerful appeal court in sport, and had had dealings with the IOC before. He was the best man for the job. Any hopes that Baxter had raised, however, were dashed when he was introduced to Beloff. The dishevelled, eccentric Oxford Don was a world away from Baxter's image of a top lawyer. He was expecting a slick, erudite man, not an unkempt professor who went off at tangents and rarely made eye contact. Beneath the veneer, however, Beloff is one of the finest legal minds in the UK and a quite brilliant QC. A lot of what he said went straight over Baxter's head but Friend could see that Beloff would be invaluable, especially if they had to take Baxter's case to appeal. But Beloff would be unable to attend the looming showdown with the IOC Inquiry Commission due to a case he was defending in the High Court. He would, however, help prepare the case and bring on board Adam Lewis, a junior barrister from Blackstone Chambers, to present Baxter's defence. Lewis came highly recommended by Beloff and the International Association of Athletics Federations (IAAF), for whom he'd done much work.

With anywhere up to two weeks to wait until the as-of-yet unscheduled IOC Inquiry Commission in Lausanne, Baxter was advised to leave the country with immediate effect. The story hadn't yet broken but it was sure to at any time. The pedestal that the nation's newspapers had built and placed Baxter upon would soon be knocked down. From Oxford, Baxter went straight to Heathrow Airport, purchased an expensive last minute flight to Norway, where he met up with girlfriend and fellow racer Pia Rivelsrud.

"I'd told Pia I needed to get away from the press but when I arrived in Geilo I told her the full story. She was shocked and we agreed not to tell her parents. I felt bad about it because they were very hospitable but I thought it was for the best. In Norway I couldn't really go many places because there were people out there that I knew. Pia still had to train because the season was still in full-swing so I'd go up with her to the slopes in disguise and pretend to be her coach. We'd ski a little bit and I'd help out with the coaching. We did a lot of cross country skiing and I went to the gym and ran a lot. I never looked for a British newspaper and I never answered my phone."

Though under strict instruction to tell no-one about the failed test, McNeilly put in a call to John Clark, who was Athlete's Representative at the BSSF but more importantly a trusted friend of both her and Baxter. Clark was on his way to present a proposal to Sport Scotland for a four-year funding and support package for

I never looked for a British newspaper or answered my phone

Lesley McKenna. McNeilly didn't need to spell it out. Clark could tell something was wrong and was stunned by the news.

"It was terrible news to get at any time but especially when I was about to ask for funding on the back of Alain's success. I sat for three hours with the Athlete's Services Coordinator, Liz Mendle, knowing what was about to hit the fan. I was hoping that the story wouldn't fully break until we'd signed-off on Lesley's funding. It was very surreal. It seemed like everything I was doing in my presentation was false. I knew that something that we'd all believed in so fervently was going to be shot down in flames. I wouldn't get to the end of my presentation. I was sitting with Meadow when the chief executive called her out of the meeting. Then all hell broke loose."

McKenna would get her funding but would have swapped every penny of it to help her cousin out of his predicament. Back in Aviemore, Baxter sent messages to his friends explaining that he had to go to London at short notice. He hated having to lie and it took all his willpower to ignore the numerous messages he got in reply. Next he called his coach. Schwaiger reacted angrily to the news. He had taken great pride in Baxter's success and knew his athlete was whiter than white. Schwaiger made him read out the ingredients of the Vick's Sinex. He was convinced it was what had caused the failed test and felt wholly responsible for Baxter's predicament.

While Baxter kept a low profile in Scandinavia the case for his defence was starting to take shape. Adam Lewis proved a valuable addition to the legal team and though their argument was still at an embryonic stage there was cause for hope. They knew that the skier had not taken Methamphetamine, they just had to figure out how to get that across to the notoriously stubborn IOC. There were three main fears that the legal team harboured, however.

Firstly, that the IOC did not distinguish between illegal Methamphetamine and exclusively medicinal Levmetamfetamine in their Anti-Doping Code – the latter was included as a 'related substance'.

Secondly, despite there being a simple test which could have demonstrated which of the two drugs Baxter had ingested, the IOC was refusing requests to carry it out.

Finally, the main concern that the legal team had was that the IOC operates a 'Strict Liability' policy for athletes. In other words, the athlete can be held responsible for anything in their system, regardless of how it got there or whether or not there was an intent to cheat.

Back in Norway Baxter was regularly updated by Sara Friend and maintained as normal a routine as possible. It was March 5. For all he knew the story could have broken back in the UK already but not merited the attention of the local press. That couldn't have been further from the truth as Baxter was about to find out.

"I was training when it all kicked-off. I was in a gym doing some sit-ups and the radio was tuned to a local station. The news came on and I thought I heard the newsreader say my name. My ears pricked up. I heard my name again and the word 'Methamphetamine', it was unmistakable. 'Here we go…' I thought. I left immediately and went to Pia's house. The first thing I did was apologise to her parents for deceiving them. They took it well. When they switched on the evening news it was one of the main items and I think they started to understand how big this was going to be. I looked at the television, transfixed, as images of my homecoming to Aviemore were shown. I could see all my friends and family. I missed them all. It seemed like a million miles away, as if it had been months ago, not days, and I wanted to be back there with them. I wondered what they thought of me? I

It seemed like a million miles away

thought of the kids waiting to see my medal back in the school in Aviemore.

"My phone started ringing constantly from then on. Later that evening we were watching a comedy show. One of the guests said he wanted to discuss Alain Baxter taking Speed. As he spoke they showed my second run from Salt Lake on fast forward, like something off the Benny Hill Show. It was surreal and in another situation could have been quite amusing. But I knew that this was just the beginning and I'd better get used to it. This story was going to be bigger than winning the medal."

THE STORY LEAKS OUT

Back in the UK after the story was leaked, curiously, in the *Dundee Courier*, and then on *Skysports*, the BOA released a statement it had prepared with Baxter before he'd left:

"Late on Friday afternoon I was telephoned by Simon Clegg, Team GB's Chef de Mission, who told me that he had been advised by the IOC's Inquiry Commission that the sample I had produced following my slalom performance at the Games contained traces of a banned substance. Naturally, I am devastated by this news.

"I have therefore decided to make public that I am the athlete in question because I have never knowingly taken any medicine or substance to improve my performance and as such believe that I am entirely innocent. I am now working with lawyers and medical experts to present my case to the IOC's Inquiry Commission (and the IOC'S Disciplinary Commission), which I am advised is unlikely to convene until next week, with a view to defending myself successfully against the charges of doping.

"I do not intend to conduct my defence through the media and as such I am not making myself available for interview and will not be making any further statement on this matter until the IOC's Inquiry and Disciplinary Commissions have ruled on my case."

Baxter wasn't required to declare that it was he who had failed the drugs test. The IOC was planning to release only his nationality and discipline at this early stage. But he felt strongly that he had nothing to hide. Nevertheless, the following day newspaper reporters, photographers, television crews and radio crews descended on Aviemore. After learning that he wasn't there, the hunt to find Baxter was on. The press pack next descended on Courchevel, where his mother was now living and working. Back in Aviemore, Baxter's family and friends continued to be hounded by the press and became virtual prisoners in their own homes. After a journalist repeatedly called Baxter's friend, Chris Helik, known in the village as 'Stork', Helik told him in no uncertain terms where to go to find Baxter. Baxter's grandfather, Chic, remembers a number of heated exchanges taking place too. They were emotional times, so soon after Baxter's homecoming parade.

"I told the BBC that it was an insult to imply that he was a drug taker when he doesn't even drink coffee when he visits me. I fell out with the *Sky News* presenter too who wouldn't accept that Alain had made a genuine mistake."

The omens weren't looking good in some pockets of the press. 'Highlander', read the headline in the *Scottish Daily Mirror*, who talked of Baxter having, 'traces of the clubber's drug speed in his system.' *The Scotsman* ran an interview with Dick Pound, an IOC member and head of the World Anti-Doping Agency (WADA). It read, 'It's the usual refrain (Baxter's plea of innocence). Have you ever heard anyone responding differently? I can think of no therapeutic use or application for Methamphetamine at all.'

THE TIDE BEGINS TO TURN

Fortunately, Baxter was saved from the waves of negative press. His only form of news was through the text messages he received and from the guestbook on his website.

"I received loads of text messages. Some friends sent jokes to cheer me up, others messages of support. The press had my number but I was told not to speak to them. I couldn't switch off my phone though because callers would have heard the Norwegian operator's message and known where I was. My website was the best way of keeping in touch with what was going on at home. The messages were overwhelmingly supportive. There were positive messages from people from all around the world. But one guy wrote,

'I knew it. It couldn't be possible for a Scot to win an Olympic medal without cheating.' Straightaway, ten replies appeared inviting the guy to go to Aviemore to repeat what he'd said in person. It was amazing to see how passionate people were. Looking back, I think I saved my sanity by not getting too involved. I kept myself to myself. I was quite strict about keeping up my training just hoping for the best outcome. It took my mind off it. I didn't seek out the newspapers at all."

Baxter's support wouldn't come exclusively from friends. After the initial frenzy died down, most of the newspapers took a balanced view of the case, many coming down in support of the skier. There was no whispering campaign, no-one was digging up any dirt on Baxter – not for the want of trying. And, far from condemning him, his fellow skiers came out in defence of the popular Scotsman. There was a quorum of support from some of the biggest names in the sport.

In *The Scotsman* on March 7, 2002, ski legend Herman Maier said, "I am very surprised, because regardless of the fact that Alain is not the sort of person I can imagine taking drugs, drugs don't really help you in skiing."

Fellow-racer Christoph Gruber, of Austria, said, "I know Alain very well and he would never take drugs. I think he should be allowed to keep the medal."

This view was echoed by the head of the Austrian Ski Team, Toni Giger, "I could not believe it, and until I see the final verdict I won't believe it. I know Alain very well, and he is the last one I would have thought would do anything like this. There must be some other explanation."

It wasn't just the skiing community that was coming out in support of Baxter. Aviemore councillor, Bob Servern, a former drugs squad officer, said in *The Scotsman*, "It doesn't make any sense. Anyone else but Alain. I have known Alain for 20 years. I've seen the work he has done and I don't believe any of this. There has to be a mistake. Everyone who knows Alain knows he does not take illegal drugs."

It seemed as if he was winning the trial by press

A further interview in *The Scotsman* quoted Dr Kurt Weingand, a source from Vick's Inhaler manufacturer, Procter & Gamble, who stated that Levmetamfetamine would have offered Baxter no performance-enhancing effects whatsoever: "We can't allow this to happen. The boy must not be punished. I am prepared to come over to tell this to the investigators."

And with the hugely influential tabloid, *The Daily Record*, staging numerous publicity stunts in support of Baxter, it seemed as if he was winning the trial by press. Even the more frothy elements of the fourth estate were getting in on the act. Despite allegedly pulling a celebratory photo spread of Baxter the day the news of the failed drugs test broke, *Hello* magazine returned to Aviemore to photograph Baxter's mother, who was now back home to lend her support to the family.

"*Hello* came to photograph me opening some of the letters that we were receiving. I thought it would be good to show that people were behind Alain. Maybe Alain, who we couldn't really speak to at that time, might see it too somehow. We were receiving letters, keepsakes, good luck charms, even some alternative brands of inhaler. Someone sent a really old ski medal from Norway. It could have even been an early Olympic medal, we were never sure. I opened one letter and an ancient coin popped out. The journalist said,

'That looks really valuable.' The letter said that it had come out of Tutankhamen's tomb. It was priceless."

Priceless too, to Baxter's future, was the work that Friend and Lewis were putting in at BOA headquarters. The controversial ex-IOC Medical Officer, Professor Arnold Beckett, had lent his weight to Baxter's defence and pointed the legal team in the right direction. Beckett knew the workings of the IOC Medical Commission better than anyone but as one of its most outspoken critics was considered to be too controversial to use as Baxter's expert witness. Instead, the BOA recruited Dr Bryan Finkle, who had more than forty years experience in the field of Forensic Toxicology and was a consultant to the IOC Medical Commission, World Anti-Doping Agency (WADA) and the US Anti-Doping Agency. Finkle carried out his own research, much of which tallied with Beckett's findings, and the defence hurriedly took shape. They would request at the IOC Inquiry that Baxter's sample be submitted to Isomer Separation Analysis to determine whether the substance found was in fact Levmetamfetamine, not Methamphetamine, which carried far more sinister undertones. If they found it to be so, it could only have

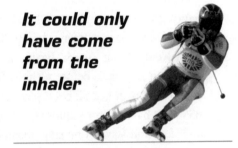

It could only have come from the inhaler

come from the inhaler. If the IOC failed to comply they would move to have charges against Baxter dropped citing the IOC's failure to conclusively prove that he had a banned substance in his body when he raced. Both arguments relied on the IOC agreeing that Levmetamfetamine had little or no stimulant properties – a hypothesis they'd backed up with expert witness statements from Finkle, Dr Weingand, of Procter & Gamble, and Dr Kadehjian, a drug abuse expert from California. A mere week had passed since the BOA had been informed of Baxter's failed test. Things were moving at breakneck speed.

Everywhere, that is, except at the IOC. The Olympic governing body was steadfastly refusing to conduct the simple test ahead of the hearing which could form the cornerstone of Baxter's defence. Simon Clegg, and BOA Chairman and IOC Member, Craig Reedie, penned multiple emails to the IOC expressing their displeasure. Reedie's complaint went directly to the top of the tree, to IOC President Jacques Rogge.

As a storm brewed at IOC HQ in Lausanne and the war of words continued in the British press, Baxter enjoyed the relative calm of Norway. He was told what he needed to know but otherwise was ordered to sit tight until the call came for him to set off for Switzerland.

"I stayed in Norway for over a week once the news broke. When Pia had to go to race I went and stayed with my old coach Rolli Johanson for four days until I had to leave. I trained there, watched TV, took time to think about what was happening. It was good catching up with Rolli, even under the circumstances. He had one word to say about it – 'Bullsh*t'."

On March 12, Baxter finally got the call he'd been waiting for. He'd have just three more days to wait before facing the IOC Inquiry and Disciplinary Commissions. On the morning of March 13, Baxter was to go to Lillehammer station and board a train to Oslo. There, he'd spend one night with the father of team-mate Gareth Trayner before flying to Zurich, where he would be met by McNeilly. From Zurich, Baxter would be driven to be reunited with his mother in Lausanne before a showdown with the most powerful governing body in sport. It had all been planned with military precision. The BOA and BSSF had handled the explosive situation with aplomb. They had thought on their feet and stayed one step ahead of the game. Baxter had made his one defining statement in absentia and spoken no more to the press. Clegg's advice to go to ground on the continent had been sage, too, saving Baxter from the relentless media intrusion and the more unsavoury views of the media ahead of his hearing. It was thought important that Baxter's state of mind when he stood before the IOC Commission was key to having any chance of saving his medal and his career.

As Baxter boarded the train in Oslo he was in a positive frame of mind. He knew the situation was serious but he was glad the waiting was over. He'd finally get the chance to put his side of the story and the case for his defence was as good as it was going to get in the short time Friend and Lewis had to construct it. Baxter even afforded himself a little optimism as he settled down for the two hour journey. As he sat there his eyes wandered around the empty carriage. It wasn't long before he noticed a newspaper that had been left behind by a previous passenger. It was an English-language newspaper. The last British papers he'd seen had announced his success at Salt Lake. It seemed like another life.

He couldn't resist picking up the paper, at least it would help pass the time. He would wish he hadn't. As he unfolded the crumpled broadsheet it became obvious that it was a well-known British daily. A familiar image greeted him on the front page. It was a picture of Baxter in full-flight at Salt Lake and it brought back so many good memories. But far from toasting his success, the headline above the photograph read, 'Speed Freak'. If Baxter was looking for a sign that the hearing would auger well, this was not it.

> CHAPTER 4   **STARTING OUT**

SEASON 1990/91
SEASON 1991/92
SEASON 1992/93
SEASON 1993/94
SEASON 1994/95
SEASON 1995/96

4   STARTING OUT

Having left school, in September 1989 Baxter started a six month course in Leisure and Recreation Management at Inverness College. The new environment was a shock to the system of the diminutive teenager. While some of his peers in the Scottish Ski Team were attending specialist skiing schools in the Alps, Baxter was mixing with trainee builders in a run-down community college. Mother, Sue, witnessed her son grow ever more insecure.

"He hated college and used to skip classes. The days he did go he'd come back in tears. A lot of the other boys there were ten years older, some had just come out of the army. Alain was only 5'2" and they could be very cruel. The teachers weren't much better. One kept calling him 'Squirt' and 'Shorty' and he would get very embarrassed."

Baxter thought about throwing in the towel on many occasions. He hadn't found the move to be the liberating experience he'd thought it would be. At least he'd never been bullied at school. Midway through the first term he was at breaking point. Baxter's mother and father were keen for their son to persevere, however. They knew that the experience would stand him in good stead in the future. Sue Dickson admits that they weren't beyond a little bribery to ensure that their son completed his course.

"We dangled a carrot to keep him there. Ian had a bike shop so we said that if he stayed until Christmas and did the work we'd get him a new bike. And he did. The following term he went back and actually enjoyed it."

The Scottish part-time Ski Team's occasional training camps provided precious respite from college life. At Christmas, Baxter travelled with the team to Austria. It would be an eye-opening experience of what life could be like on the road with older skiers. Baxter would be the youngest skier in the team for the foreseeable future.

"I had two good weeks of training before we went to Jerzens to race. I was small but I was as fit and strong as anyone on the team. It was New Year's Eve and the town was really busy so the coaches were in a different hotel to us.

The night before the race one of the older boys found a bottle of vodka in the cellar, which was just next to the ski room. He got some Coke and someone said, 'Hey Baxter, try some of this.' I'd never drunk alcohol before. We started playing drinking games and I had no idea what was going on. Luckily my skis had been prepared for the next day because I was on a different planet. I stayed up all night being sick. In the minibus the next morning, our coach was sitting behind me and I was looking out of the window thinking, 'I'm going to be sick any minute!' While inspecting the course before the race I had to run off into the woods and throw up. I said there and then that I'd never drink before a race again. I actually came 11th. I'll never know how because I'd been banging into things all morning."

The young skier arrived back from his mind-broadening trip to the harsh reality of college life but applied himself well and picked up a handful of qualifications. He left in March 1990 more confident and self-assured than when he'd started. Soon after Baxter was offered the chance to become a joiner's apprentice. The offer stumped Baxter briefly. It was his second-choice career. It fell to mum, Sue, to provide some sage advice:

I had to run off into the woods and throw up

"I told him if he was to ski he had to do it now. He could be a joiner when he was 35. He nodded. 'Okay then.'"

It was the decision Baxter would have ultimately reached anyway. As cousin Lesley points out, he'd been preparing for it all his life.

"The prospect of making a career out of skiing wasn't foreign to Alain. He didn't get to 16 and say, 'I really want to be a ski racer but the other guys are so good, and I'm from Scotland and I've got no money so it's going to take so much sacrifice.' That didn't even enter Alain's head. He was already thinking like the guys who were the best in the world in his age group."

Mind made up, the pragmatic young Scot knew he would have to take every opportunity to spend time on the snow before the following season. A happy coincidence enabled Baxter to ski uninterrupted for several weeks in early spring before joining up with the team for the British Junior

Championships. Baxter travelled to Val d'Isere with his aunt and uncle, who were building a chalet in the resort. Baxter was able to ski in the morning with cousin Ross and train with a group of French racers every afternoon. He soon noticed the difference:

"At the British Juniors in Val Morel the races were difficult because some of the Senior team were still eligible to compete but I did okay. I was still small but people had noticed that I was skiing better than I had at Christmas. I had been out getting in miles on the snow while most of the guys I was competing against were still in school."

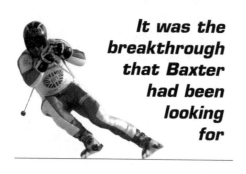

It was the breakthrough that Baxter had been looking for

Baxter did better than 'okay'. He came 7th in the Super G, though he was younger than all those ahead of him by up to two years. He was 10th in the GS, beaten by only one skier younger than him, and finished 16th in the Slalom. It was the breakthrough that Baxter had been looking for and the results attracted the attention of team bosses at the newly-formed Scottish Alpine-based Team, who recruited Baxter for the 1990/91 season.

SEASON: 1990/91

Age: 16/17
Team: Scottish Alpine-based Team
World Ranking (Slalom): unranked

Baxter's season started with him and his mother painstakingly putting together a sponsorship portfolio. It outlined his aims, achievements and funding requirement for the coming season. Baxter needed to raise £950 for a training camp in Austria and considerably more for the season proper. It was an official Scottish Team but funding was non-existent. If a skier wanted to join the team, they were expected to pay their own way. If the team wanted a coach, they had to pay for it themselves. As it would be his first season, certain costs that he and his mother estimated were out by some way. Below is a break down of the projected costs (with actual costs in brackets).

SCOTTISH ALPINE-BASED SKI TEAM (1990/91)

Trainers fees	£900	(£1,200)
Food & Accommodation (27 weeks, £25 per day)	£1,100	(£4,900)
Insurance	£300	(£550)
Race Entries	£130	(£200)
Lift passes	£180	(£350)
Petrol	£150	(£1,000)
Flights, trains, ferries	£800	(£500)
Skis x 4	£1,520	(£1,520)
Total	**£5,080**	**(£10,220)**

Baxter's mother was shocked at the prospect that they'd have to raise £5,000 (it was nothing compared to the sheer panic when she later realised her son had spent double that figure). It became clear that Baxter's dream hung in the balance unless sponsors could be found, and found quickly. While his mother fretted, Baxter worked every hour god sent in the local swimming pool. He'd do odd jobs too and never turned down the chance to earn a few pounds. He saved every penny he earned and gradually the money started mounting up.

Baxter's dream hung in the balance

"I worked all summer, the training camp aside, and funding was slowly falling into place. I got £250 from the Sports Council and Hans Kuwall, an Austrian ski instructor who ran the Carrbridge Ski School, offered to cover my accommodation. I couldn't have afforded that season without him. It was humbling and I was determined not to waste the opportunity."

The Hintertux training camp was set up by ex-racer, Nigel Smith, Claire

Weight training in the early years

Booth and Kuwall with the help of the Aberdeen Ski Club and Hugh Robertson of Hanson & Robertson Insurance. Robertson had two daughters who raced and it was through them that he had made Baxter's acquaintance. He offered to help the young skier pay for the camp when he learnt he was having problems. Robertson was a self-made man. He'd started selling insurance door-to-door and went on to become one of the market leaders. Yet he remained down to earth. He saw a bit of himself in Baxter. His never-say-die attitude, combined with a gentle manner endeared him to the businessman and it would be the start of a long relationship which would also see Robertson become Baxter's occasional summer employer.

Robertson's help allowed Baxter to concentrate on skiing. The team trained on a glacier for six weeks with coach, Ernst Trenkwalder. Trenkwalder put as much emphasis on training off the snow as on, subjecting the team to a punishing fitness regime. It was not wasted on Baxter who was eager to learn. If that's what it took to improve as a skier, that's what he would do. Baxter responded well to the race training too, coming on in leaps and bounds. He was as fast as any of the older skiers. Trenkwalder would also teach the team tricks, and always found a willing volunteer in the fearless Scot. He mastered the somersault on his second attempt. The team would also be expected to participate in running, skating and tree climbing competitions. Baxter found light relief away from the camp too.

"We lived with a local family on the top floor of their house. It was like a scene from Heidi. We had fresh milk every morning straight from the cows. You didn't even have to heat it up for hot chocolate."

Baxter was living the dream and, after returning home, counted down the days, as carefully as his mother counted up the pounds raised through various fund-raising initiatives, until he could rejoin the team. The Scottish Alpine-based Team was the first serious attempt to give young Scottish skiers the chance to catch up with their foreign counterparts. Whereas Britain would struggle to find one international level skier, Austria could recruit a world-class team from every village. There were ski academies on every glacier and the country had thousands of skiers to chose from, while Britain had hundreds. It was so far behind that it would take years of exposure to the international circuit for a British skier to establish themself, let alone get in a position to challenge for podiums. But therein lay the rub. While the majority of top foreign skiers Baxter's age were being fully-funded by their ski federations or were given token jobs in the Army or Forestry Commission, Baxter received no government funding. He was prepared for the hard slog to climb the rankings but whether he would continue, season after season, to be able to raise the money to allow him to get to a stage where he could compete with the best was another matter. It would be a case of survival of the fittest.

There is no free ride in international skiing. Whether you race Downhill, where speed is king, or the highly technical disciplines like Slalom and Giant Slalom (GS), or the slightly elongated Super G, you start at the bottom and work your way up. The entry level for international racers is the lowly Citaden Tour or the slightly tougher FIS (International Ski Federation) Race circuit. From there it is on to the more prestigious Europa and Nor-Am Cup tours. Skiers must improve their world ranking sufficiently before being allowed to compete at the next level. Baxter would have to progressively earn his stripes at these lower tier events until his ranking was sufficient to allow him to join the hallowed World Cup circuit. As an affiliated member of FIS, Britain is eligible to send one skier to each World Cup Race, but only if they are of suitable standard. With only ten to twelve races per season, and only the top 75 skiers eligible to compete, it is skiing's Champion's League. It culminates with the World Cup Finals, where the top skiers in each discipline race to decide their champions. It is the holy grail for racers, only surpassed by the bi-annual World Championships and the Olympics. But Baxter had a long way to go. He was unranked with 6,000 skiers ahead of him and he was just about to have his first taste of senior international racing. It is a race he'll never forget.

"I got a big shock. I was near the top of the pile in Britain and then I went out into the real world. Standing at the start of my first big race, starting 140th (last) in the field, I was having second thoughts, thinking, 'What have I let myself in for?' It was extremely nerve wracking."

But Baxter posted a respectable 45th place in the low-ranking FIS Slalom race and went on to compete in three FIS Giant Slalom (GS) races by late February, posting top 50 finishes in each. It would be the extent of his international races that year, turning his attention back to the British Championships in March where he finished 6th (Slalom), and the British Junior Championships – for which he was still eligible – where he finished 2nd (GS) and 5th (Super G).

The most valuable lesson that Baxter learnt that year was the importance of consistency. As the season wore on, Baxter started having problems finishing races. At the British Juniors he had been leading by two seconds but stormed down the second run recklessly, crashing out. It wasn't in his nature to risk coming DFL, as the team called it – Dead F**king Last. There was no worse ignominy. But he knew that he couldn't go on as he was, so put more thought into skiing tactically. It seemed to work and Baxter didn't lose as much speed as he'd expected. Baxter's claim to fame is that he has never been last in a race.

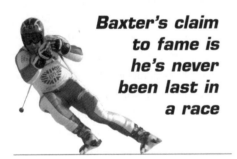

Baxter's claim to fame is he's never been last in a race

Life on the road was far-removed from Baxter's settled childhood in the Highlands. He was travelling thousands of miles a month, living out of a suitcase, learning to look after himself. He also learnt that there were more hazards in life than a tight Slalom gate and got an insight into ex-racer Trenkwalder's calm under pressure, a quality required by all good racers.

"One day our bus went into a massive spin on an Alpine pass. We were travelling backwards at 60mph in the middle lane of a three lane carriageway. I looked over at Ernst to see what he was going to do – Danny Maddox was driving – and he looked up from his book, cool as you like, and started to yodel. I thought 'Sh*t, we're done for now?' We stopped on the hard shoulder after a few more spins and all fell straight on our backsides when we jumped out because it was so icy. Ernst just sat there reading his book."

Baxter was happy with his debut season. He'd spent six months on the snow and was ranked for the first time: 1372 for Slalom, which would become his chosen discipline, 1495 for Super G and 1599 for GS. It may not have seemed like progress but for Baxter it had been worth every night in budget accommodation, every one of the thousands of pounds that he was overdrawn.

I just scraped by... the funding situation was bad

"That whole season I just scraped by. The funding situation was bad but, truthfully, it didn't bother me. I just kept on writing the Eurocheques and worried about it when I got home. We weren't all like that on the team. Mark Tilston had to give up. He couldn't afford it. What kept me going was that towards the end of the season I started putting some distance between myself and the others. I was the only skier from that group who would make it to the next level."

The season held a final bonus for the 17-year-old. Baxter was selected to go to the World Junior Championships in Hemsedal, Norway. It would be the biggest race of Baxter's career and after a mammoth bus journey from France to Norway, via Aviemore, Baxter finished 46th. It was good but Baxter still had a long way to go to be where he wanted to be.

SEASON: 1991/92

Age: 17/18
Team: British Development Team
World Ranking (Slalom): 1372

Baxter returned to Aviemore knowing he needed to earn money fast and landed a job as a gardener. The next stage in Baxter's development as a skier would be to attain a place in the British Development Team, a feeder-squad for the seniors. Baxter's good showing at the British Championships had caught the eyes of the selectors as had his top 50 finish at the World Juniors and he was invited to join up with the Development Team in Altenmarkt, Austria, in October. Again, Baxter would be the youngest member of the team.

Baxter had high hopes for the season and expected to have access to coaching and support that he could only have dreamt about the year before.

The younger skiers were completely self-funding

It couldn't have been further from the truth. The BSSF was not a rich organisation. Any funding that it did receive from the Sports Council or sponsors was spent on its top skiers. It came as a shock to Baxter.

"All we got given was the status, a skisuit, goggles, gloves, hat and a telephone number to ring to enter races. There was no coach, no transport, no accommodation – nothing. We had to run the team ourselves."

Fiona McNeilly, who joined as Alpine Secretary at the BSSF in 1993, recalls that the lack of funding was a constant bone of contention in Baxter's early days on the team.

"Even our top skiers, Graham and Martin Bell, were getting absolutely minimal funding in the early 1990s. They were paying for many of their own flights and expenses but got full coaching support and funding to go to World Cups, assuming there was money in the Federation coffers. The younger skiers were completely self-funding."

£8,700 was the bare minimum that Baxter needed to raise to fund the season. It was marginally less than what he'd spent the season before because he'd have no coach. He and his mother sat down to put together a sponsorship appeal for the season. In it, Baxter spoke of a specific goal: "…to win the British Junior Championships."

Again, Baxter somehow managed to scrape together enough sponsorship, grants and savings to fund the season. In these early years Baxter would be sponsored at various stages by Ryden Property, The Aviemore Brewery and Hanson & Robertson Insurance. It would be critical because the season would be like no other for Baxter. Faced with such a lack of support, having his own transport would be key. Baxter's mother taught him to drive that summer and gave him his first car.

"When Alain was learning to drive we had 'Betsy', a mark one VW Passat Estate. But he could barely see over the steering wheel and drove off the road on a few occasions, so we traded it in for something smaller. Alain passed his test with ease. When winter came he needed a car to travel to the Alps and we noticed that Betsy was still sitting at the local garage. It was a real banger but we couldn't afford anything else so we got it back."

That it was a banger is not in doubt. Baxter's father remembers taking the car to a local mechanic for the once-over.

"I said 'Geordie, what do you think?' He replied, 'It could make it to Kingussie (ten miles south of Aviemore). Or it could go to the Alps and back. Or it might not even reach Kingussie.'"

The Passat was a patchwork quilt of spare parts but to Baxter it represented freedom.

"It was 12 years old but I thought it was a beauty. It was blue with one brown door and had a massive hole in the boot. You could see clear daylight where it had rusted, and this was before a season in the snow. The handbrake was temperamental too, which wasn't ideal for the Alps."

But the car would take Baxter all the way to the temporary team base in Altenmarkt. He was becoming accustomed to the supreme efforts he had to face to even make it to the start line of international races. But far from being the laughing stock of the circuit, Baxter feels that the unsupported team gained the respect of their better-funded rivals.

"Most of the foreign skiers had new cars, coaches, physios, and we were driving around in bangers with one set of kit, but we were never a joke. Mostly because they could see that we could actually ski."

Lesley McKenna, who was becoming increasingly disgruntled at the lack of support she was receiving in her own blossoming career as a Downhill racer, is full of admiration for how her cousin approached the season.

"Alain worked with the tools that he had. He accepted the situation and knew that it would get better. The important thing was that he got as many hours on snow as he could afford. Nothing else mattered. A different type of person might have said, 'I need to go to every FIS race, I need a coach, I need a trainer, I need a physio, I need a serviceman but I can't afford any of it so

I'm not going to do it at all.' But Alain looked at the situation and knew what had to be done. He knew all those things would be good but he concentrated on what he could do. Many others quit because they couldn't live with the sacrifices."

Despite being the paupers of the international scene, Baxter and teammates Scott Ballantine, Mike Rowe, Roger Hughes, Marjory Adams, Adam Sullivan, Dan Walker, Roger Walker and Andrew Freshwater approached the season with gusto. They had two cars and a van and covered 11,000 miles, criss-crossing the Alps. Austria made for a good base as it was within easy reach of many races and because accommodation was cheap. This didn't stop the team squeezing into single hotel rooms on occasion. Sometimes even that would seem palatial:

"Once we went to Italy for a Citaden race. We arrived late and there was no chance to get a hotel, even if we could have afforded it. So we parked up, got in our sleeping bags, and tried to sleep. It was freezing. We'd parked next to the chairlift and in the morning as the other teams were driven up, fresh from a good night's sleep, a hot shower, and a massage, there was us stood in our boxer shorts in the snow, putting on our long johns and ski suits. Amazingly I finished 9th and came 10th in the next race."

It wouldn't be the last night Baxter spent in his car that season. Between the rapidly disintegrating Passat and Freshwater's van Baxter would spend numerous nights shivering in his sleeping bag, thinking of his rivals tucked-up in their warm hotels. But Baxter was undeterred. Indeed it drove him on. He never lost sight of his goal because he was beginning to perform and, despite the absence of a coach, was learning with every race. He may not have been beating many people in races but in practice they could see that the Scot had an abundance of raw potential.

Though he wasn't doing as many races as he would have liked, Baxter did well in those he entered and his ranking was constantly improving. Come March the British Championships offered him the chance to race against members of the senior team. It was the best yardstick to measure his progress. Despite crashing out of the Slalom, Baxter finished 8th in the Super G and 9th in the Downhill. It was another watershed result, especially as he hoped to graduate to the senior team the following season.

The British Juniors were even more successful. Baxter almost fulfilled his season goal, winning the GS and Super G but, much to his disgust, again crashed out from a winning position in the Slalom. Nevertheless, Baxter had done enough to be selected for the World Junior Championships, in Maribor, Yugoslavia. Baxter spent a week in Courchevel with his mother and stepfather before leaving for Maribor.

"Alain left on Tuesday and the Federation called on Friday to ask where he was. We were a bit worried. Up until then he had navigated himself around Europe really well. Sometimes he'd get the map out and say, 'OK, where's Italy?' but he always got there in the end. So this was a bit of a concern, especially as there was a civil war going on in parts of Yugoslavia."

Unbeknown to his mother, Baxter hadn't even made it through Austria. His windscreen wipers had died during a snowstorm and he had to clear his windscreen by hand for several frantic miles before reaching Ernst Trenkwalder's village. Trenkwalder invited Baxter to stay and train with his talented group of young Austrians. Ever hungry to challenge himself, Baxter accepted. He also travelled with the team to a high level race nearby and put in a good account of himself. But it would take Baxter longer than anticipated to reach Maribor. His wipers would fail repeatedly, and when a tunnel tollbooth attendant refused Baxter's Eurocheque, he spent hours searching his car and luggage, finally paying the vital toll in low denomination coins from three currencies.

Baxter finally arrived to find that he'd caused a widespread panic. Whether it was worth the journey is open to debate.

"I was skiing well after training with Ernst. He'd noticed that I'd grown a lot and it gave my confidence a boost. But I started the Slalom in the high fifties by which time there was grass in the ruts and I didn't complete the course. I didn't really mature early enough for the World Juniors, though. I just hadn't raced at a high enough level."

Baxter's disappointment would be short-lived. He'd had a good season, slashing his Slalom ranking to 960 and was named KPMG Scottish Skier of the Year. Baxter was pleased with the accolade but was only truly content when he was selected for the British Team for the 1992/93 season. Baxter's upward trajectory was continuing better than he could have expected.

SEASON: 1992/93

Age: 18/19
Team: British Team
World Ranking (Slalom): 960

Baxter had taken to life on the road like a duck to water but he was always glad to return home. However, the demands of being in the British Team required him to spend more and more time away from the village. This also meant that he had less time to work. When he was able, he worked in the Ellis Brigham outdoor store, but his portfolio for that year saw Baxter seeking £7,100, not including the two summer camps in Norway or the coaching fees, which would be paid for by Hanson & Robertson. He remembers distinctly that preparation and team support moved up a notch when he joined the new team.

"That season things really started to take shape for me. Jorn Kasine, who had been Norwegian World Cup coach, was brought over to help Nigel Smith. Jorn was fresh to the scene and brought a lot of knowledge and experience. The camps in Norway were really good because we trained with the Norwegian team, who were head and shoulders above us. I was responding to the coaching and had never felt so good going into a season."

The team started the season out in Norway too. They did twenty races on the competitive domestic circuit against World Cup-standard skiers. Winning races was not realistic for any of the young team. Instead Baxter, Dan and Roger Walker, David Cook, Mike Rowe and Adam Sullivan scrapped for valuable ranking points.

After Christmas in Aviemore, Baxter drove back to the Alps. The team never flew between events because they couldn't afford it and they didn't have a permanent base that year, instead staying in budget accommodation or relying on the generosity of ex-pat Brits. More than specific results, Baxter remembers making real progress in training and of starting to feel like he belonged on the same piste as world class racers.

Baxter was finally competing on a level playing field

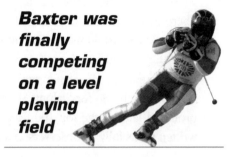

"I started to get better and better. I still wasn't doing much in international races but I was catching up with the top guys in the British team. It was a combination of having far better coaching but also finally getting better skis."

Whereas Baxter had always raced on mass-produced skis, Kasine's contacts with the manufacturers gave him access, for the first time, to Factory or Race Department skis, which were tailor-made for racers. Baxter was finally competing on a level playing field with his foreign counterparts, who'd used the skis all their careers. Unlike them, however, Baxter was still required to service and prepare his own skis. Something a top young Austrian racer was never likely to have done.

"I'd have to do my skis every day. They had to be well-waxed, the edges smooth and sharp – I was a real perfectionist. I learnt a lot about the equipment. There are angles everywhere: on the side of the ski, the bottom of the ski; then there's the flex of the ski, torsion, ramp angles in your plates, in your boots, height underneath your boot, wedges in the back of your boot, in the front of your boot. It's a real science. It could take hours to get them just right and we'd often have to borrow tools from the local sports shop but we knew we had to do it. Most of the other skiers would have everything mounted for them and someone preparing their skis. I didn't get my own serviceman until 2001."

At the British Championships that spring Baxter got the chance to show how much he'd improved. He was confident and was going faster than ever before. He finished 5th in both the GS and Super G, 7th in the Downhill and an impressive 2nd in the Slalom, to round off his best ever Championships. There was a growing feeling in the ski community that it wouldn't be long before Baxter would usurp his senior team-mates.

1992/93 would be the season when Baxter would gain most places in the World Rankings. He leap-frogged an astonishing 574 skiers to finish the season ranked 386 for Slalom. Slowly but surely he was edging towards the promised land of the top 100. Hoping for anything more would have been written off as folly by observers, but not Baxter.

SEASON: 1993/94

Age: 19/20
World Ranking (Slalom): 386

In 1993 Baxter again spent his summer between Norway, at two gruelling camps, and Aviemore. Whilst at home, Baxter worked in Aberdeen for Hanson & Robertson Insurance doing renewals until a series of errors was discovered and he was moved out of harm's way to scan files. It would be Baxter's one and only office job, arranged by Hugh Robertson.

"If it wasn't for people like Hugh, I wouldn't have been able to do it. It's as simple as that. If he hadn't helped me out in those early years I would have been stuck. He never said why he sponsored me. I guess he's just a genuine guy with a big heart. He said that the day after I won my Olympic medal he had the biggest hangover of his life."

Summer training was no walk in the park. Baxter trained six days a week, four hours a day, on top of working and playing ice hockey. In an ideal world he would have trained full-time like his European counterparts but it wasn't an option for the cash-strapped Scot. Baxter was self-funding a large portion of his season so it was critical that he worked. McNeilly has an abiding memory of Baxter at this pivotal stage of his development.

"If you work with athletes long enough you can begin to tell which ones are going to make it. There's always an element of egotism but sometimes you get an unnecessary arrogance. Not Alain. He was extremely focused. There were those who would give financial reasons for excusing themselves from training camps but Alain never once said that. He would be knocking in fence posts until an hour before we left if that's what it took."

McNeilly's arrival at the Federation marked the first phase of its streamlining. Funding from the Sports Council was under threat and, despite operating a zero-budget, the Federation was well-populated with administrators. There were eight staff when McNeilly joined, which was soon whittled down to three. The team was also too large. There were 200 registered racers, with 40 regularly competing, and even the Federation admitted that they were lucky if they had five international standard athletes.

Part of the 'problem' was that sponsorship from Drambuie had allowed the Federation to support a disproportionately large team for such a small skiing nation. When Drambuie pulled out it had to change. 1993 would be the first year that the Federation would slim down the team to focus on its elite athletes. It would take three years before this policy was fully implemented and in the interceding years Baxter would see team-mate after team-mate culled. Fortunately, Baxter's star was in the ascendancy. He started the season with a bang, coming 1st, 4th, 5th and 1st in the first four Citaden GS Races. The run of results was far and above anything the Scot had achieved before.

Though the team had far more structure than Baxter had been used to, there were still times when he'd have to find his own way to races. On these occasions McNeilly prepared herself for the inevitable call.

"Alain would say, 'I'm supposed to be in Austria tomorrow. Have you booked me a hotel?' I'd say, 'Did you ask me to?' Alain would sound sheepish, 'No, could you do it now?' I always did, of course, and he always made me feel appreciated, bringing me the occasional bottle of gin from Duty Free. Some of the others acted like prima donnas, like it was their right to trample all over the administrators."

McNeilly was agony aunt and love life facilitator for many of the young skiers. Baxter dated fellow-skier Emma Carrick-Anderson for four years and would often ask McNeilly to coordinate a teleconference so the two could speak. It highlighted the difficulty for Baxter to have any sort of conventional relationship during the season, even with another skier. The advent of mobile phones would make life easier for everyone in the team.

In January, Baxter continued his excellent run of form finishing 5th, his best FIS Race result, in Kirchberg, Austria. It was perfect preparation for the British Championships later that month. All eyes were on Baxter at the event, especially those of his older team-mates who felt the young Scot breathing down their necks. They'd all soon be scrapping for what little funding was available. Unfortunately Baxter could go no better than his 2nd place of the year before in the Slalom but finally cemented his arrival on the

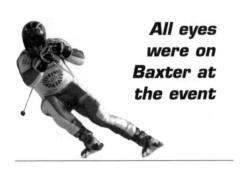

All eyes were on Baxter at the event

senior scene by winning the GS in impressive style. The result was enough to see Baxter crowned overall Champion.

Baxter used the result as a springboard for further success. In his next six FIS Races he was 2nd (GS), 8th (Slalom), 8th (GS), 11th (GS), 10th (GS), and 4th (GS). It was an enviable string of results and Baxter only just failed to fulfil Colin Grant's prophecy from six years before by missing out on selection for the 1994 Winter Olympics in Lillehammer. Undeterred Baxter recorded back-to-back victories in his final two FIS Races of the season, finishing above the Bell brothers, who were travelling to Lillehammer.

Baxter drove back at the end of the season with Smith and Freshwater. It was a mammoth journey and to save time the three would take turns driving. While one drove, the other two would sleep on the make-shift bed of rucksacks in the back of the van. After five hours they would switch, while the van was moving, to save time. The gruelling journey took its toll on Baxter who, while still half asleep, filled up the diesel van with petrol. His punishment was to have to stay awake for hours making small-talk to the AA driver who arrived to tow them back to the BSSF office in Edinburgh. Baxter was dead on his feet upon arrival at 6am.

"We had nowhere to go so Nigel let us in and left. We found loads of old ski jackets in a cupboard, piled them on the ground and went to sleep for most of the day. By this point we could have slept anywhere. Probably not the best preparation for elite athletes but we were happy to be doing what we loved."

The preparation may have been suspect but Baxter's progress was not. He finished the season ranked 301 for Slalom and 178 for GS, a staggering leap of 735 places. It was another milestone, being the first time Baxter had entered the top 200.

SEASON: 1994/95

Age: 20/21
World Ranking (Slalom): 301

Summers were taking on a familiar bent for Baxter. He'd train, ski on the glacier in Norway, and tick off the days until the start of the season. Hugh Robertson had learned that Baxter was best kept away from the office and hired him as a gardener that summer. But he was no more convinced that it was Baxter's calling after he accidentally cut the tail off one of his prized peacocks. Robertson was again part-funding Baxter for the season but a portfolio from the time, omitting summer training camp costs, showed that the Scot needed to raise £9,900 for the 32 week season.

At least Baxter was finally getting full coaching support from the BSSF. Swede Rolli Johanson took over from Kasine and Smith, and Baxter was looking forward to his fifth season as a racer. With a substantially improved ranking, the plan was for Baxter to enter higher quality races. He'd need to start earning better world ranking points if he was ever going to step up to the next level. Ranking points are awarded depending on how well a skier does in a race, and by how good the other skiers in that race are. For example, it would be better for Baxter to finish 10th in a Europa Cup against a better field, than 3rd in a lowly Citaden race.

Baxter started the season inauspiciously, straddling a gate on his second run of a FIS GS race in Norway. Straddling is when a racer skis with one ski either side of a pole, rather than around it. It is caused by a minute miscalculation and is the skiing equivalent of the dreaded golfer's 'Yips'. He failed to finish his next FIS Race too but finished 39th (Super G) and 23rd (Slalom), respectively, thereafter. In December, Baxter entered a further nine races – four FIS and five Europa Cup – only finishing twice: 23rd (FIS Slalom) and 20th (FIS GS). It wasn't the start to the season that he had hoped for but he knew that it was time to make the step up, even if his results did briefly suffer. Finishing would be a start.

After Christmas, Baxter returned determined to be more consistent. Despite the psychological impact of becoming prone to straddling, he was also preoccupied by the fact that he was spending lots of money attending races but winning no ranking points. And he made a poor start to the year, failing to finish three of his first four FIS races. He finished a much-needed 10th in the race he did finish and would post a confidence-boosting 3rd place in the very next race in Hakadal, Norway. Buoyed by this, Baxter's confidence began to return.

By February Baxter seemed to have exorcised the demons but had a lot of work to do to rescue his ranking. For the first time he raced in the Far East Cup, the Asian equivalent of the Europa Cup. In Yong Pyeong, South Korea, Baxter was 35th (GS) and 22nd (Slalom). From thereon in his season improved. He started to consistently finish races but there was no discernible pattern to his results. He finished 13th (GS), 42nd (Super G), 18th (Super G) and 20th (GS) yet it didn't feel like the great leap forward of the season before. Then he'd actually won races, albeit lower ranking. To the casual observer it may have appeared that Baxter had reached a plateau.

In early March he crashed out or straddled in four out of eight races, finishing 26th (GS), 17th (Slalom), 10th (GS) and 18th (GS) in those he did complete. It wasn't perfect preparation for the British Championships. There, Baxter failed to finish the Slalom, was 2nd in the GS and 5th in the Super G. It wasn't a terrible showing but Baxter should have been winning all three. It was the kick up the backside that he needed. At the French Championships Baxter made it onto the podium twice against an excellent field. It got his season back on track just in time. There were five crucial FIS races left. Though Baxter couldn't avoid recording a DNF1 (did not finish 1st run) in two of the five, he did finish 10th (GS) at Puy Saint Vincent, France, and 2nd (GS) and 1st (Slalom) at Aonach Mor, Scotland.

Baxter's string of good results at the end of the season had been important to make sure that his world rankings were preserved. They did slip slightly, however, in Slalom, which he'd done less of, to 383, and GS to 219.

Effectively it had been a year of treading water for the Scot. It was a reality check and he, literally, couldn't afford another season like it.

SEASON: 1995/96

Age: 21/22
World Ranking (Slalom): 383

In the summer of 1995, Baxter trained maniacally at home and in Norway. It would cost Baxter, his long-suffering bank manager, and his sponsors £15,000-plus per season now he intended to attend more races. Hanson & Robertson remained a faithful sponsor and Baxter worked for Robertson again. Having an understanding employer was key to Baxter's ability to keep up his strict regime. He started his season in Bjorli, Norway, with a respectable 27th and 21st (both GS) in two FIS Races. He finished 21st (Slalom) in nearby Geilo but the next two races would see the Scot crash. Baxter bounced back in the next race, finishing 8th, and his results began to become harder to predict than the weather in his native Aviemore.

Baxter limped through to Christmas indifferently, never managing a top ten result. January was no different. He either straddled, or finished way down the field in races. He failed to post a result in any of the seven Europa Cups that season. February was a nadir for the skier. Starting reasonably well, finishing 20th and 32nd in two FIS GS Races in Alpe D'Huez, Baxter's form deteriorated further and he only finished two of the next seven races. The silver lining to the dark cloud which hung over him was that one of those races was his first ever World Ski Championships, in Sierra Nevada, Spain. Baxter's 26th place in a world class field was a spectacular result, proving that he had what it took to compete on the big stage. The problem remained, however, that if Baxter failed to correct his downward spiral he would never get his ranking low enough to ski there again.

Baxter was briefly rejuvenated after the World Championships. He was 3rd in a FIS Race in Scotland before returning to the Alps to compete in seven FIS Races and one Europa Cup. He only finished in the top 20 once. Frustration was setting in.

"I was trying my hardest and getting nothing from it, feeling as if I was banging my head against a brick wall. My results were going backwards for the first time and I got pretty depressed with the situation. My Slalom ranking was slipping and it went down as far as 592 prior to Sierra Nevada."

It wasn't only Baxter's skiing that was deteriorating. McKenna, who was in the same squad, felt that the whole team was unravelling.

"It was terrible, so bad that I quit. There was no money, everybody was fighting, it was the worst a team could get. Everything that could go wrong went wrong. It was frustrating because I knew that I couldn't get to where I wanted to be in that set up and Alain felt the same."

Come late March, Baxter's patience was wearing wafer thin. Skiing felt like a slog for the first time. It was all he could do to get himself fired-up for the British Championships. Baxter finished 1st (GS), 3rd (Super G), and 4th (Slalom) to win the overall title but, far from celebrating, the result caused him to take a long, hard look at himself.

"I knew that wasn't good enough. I was the best in Britain but I didn't feel at that moment in time that I was ever going to achieve anything on the international scene."

Baxter's self-analysis was uncharacteristic. He'd never questioned his path before, but after failing to finish two-thirds of the remaining races that season he was staring into a black hole. His ranking had taken a beating. His Slalom ranking had slipped 55 places to 438 and his GS ranking had nearly doubled to 432. Baxter was going backwards. Things seemed to have come full-circle, especially after a chance meeting with some old friends.

"I met Fraser and Bridget Clyde, who had got me into racing all those years before. I told them I was at the end of my tether. I'd had enough. I couldn't see it going further. They said to me, 'You can't quit. Just give it a bit of time.' But I was skint, I was skiing badly, and my heart wasn't in it anymore."

Baxter returned to Aviemore with a lot of thinking to do. Father, Ian, was steadfast in his advice:

"I told Alain to have a break before making a decision. He'd known that there were going to be hard times and I knew how frustrated he was but I felt that he was on the verge of making a breakthrough."

As the summer dragged on, Baxter spent his days working in the local ice rink. In the evenings he drank. By his own admission he went off the rails.

"For a couple of weeks I didn't really know what was going on. I wanted to enjoy home life a bit more. I saw that my mates were all happy studying or working. It looked like good fun compared to what I was going through. I did still train and I learnt to do backflips in the gym. I showed my mates in the pub and landed at a weird angle and broke my toe. It didn't do my state of mind any good. All I could think about was that everything I'd ever done, ever known, seemed to be coming to an end."

Baxter even considered switching to snowboarding. He had introduced his cousin, Lesley, to the sport, in which she'd go on to excel. He was also offered a contract to play ice hockey in the British Superleague. He was tempted by both routes, but he couldn't get out of his mind all the hard work he'd put in, all the sacrifices he'd made. It was the toughest decision of his life but he'd always told himself that if his progress halted he would call it a day. There was no shame in it. So many other British skiers had reached the same point.

When Baxter excused himself from a training camp for the first time in his career, it set alarm bells ringing at the BSSF. Baxter told them he wanted to quit but the Federation was unequivocal: he was their number one skier and they didn't want to lose him. By the time Baxter was summoned to meet with the Federation, he'd had time to reflect. He realised that he'd made little progress under the coaching structure in recent years, and felt he was nowhere near fulfilling his potential. Baxter had thought long and hard about his future and came to a decision. Despite it not being in his nature to rock the boat, drastic action was needed – he'd issue an ultimatum. In no uncertain terms Baxter told the Federation to bring in a coach who could take him on to the next level or he was gone.

> CHAPTER 5   **THE FIGHT BEGINS**

PREPARING THE CASE
FACING THE IOC
SWIMMING AGAINST THE TIDE
A VERY PERSONAL TESTIMONY
AWAITING THE VERDICT
THE SUPPORT BUILDS

5   THE FIGHT BEGINS

Baxter's guardian angel was there to meet him when he touched down in Zurich. Fiona McNeilly had met the Snowboard Team in Geneva, taken their car and spent hours painstakingly removing any team or sponsor regalia from the exterior. It had been as cloak and dagger as Baxter's dawn flight from the Highlands. The pair, who had been through so much together, drove from Zurich to Lausanne. It was a well-trodden path for the skier, knowing every mile of every road in the region. In Lausanne, Baxter was reunited with his mother and stepfather for the first time since Clegg's call had set off the sorry series of events. The BOA had checked Baxter's family into an out-of-the-way hotel in an effort to evade the press.

"It was a very emotional reunion. I'd felt like a fugitive during the previous two weeks and hadn't been able to speak to my family at all, so it was good to see them again. It was the first time I'd seen Kenny at all since winning the medal and I got the feeling all he really wanted to do was congratulate me and make all the other stuff disappear. It was funny because I was used to being away from them for months on end but I'd never been more glad to see their faces. It felt like I'd been away for an eternity. They had hundreds of letters of support and gifts and good luck charms from people. It felt great to see that I had support at home and not just from family and friends."

PREPARING THE CASE

After dinner, Baxter met with Friend and Lewis to go over the following day's proceedings. They laid out their arguments explaining the theory and legal context of each one. It was too simplistic to plead his innocence on the basis that he had merely used a Vick's Inhaler and inadvertently ingested a banned substance. The IOC's 'Strict Liability' policy meant athletes were responsible for anything found in their bodies, regardless of how it got there. Baxter's team would have to focus on whether the substance found was indeed what the IOC claimed it was, and if it was not, that Baxter should be exonerated. It all sounded very promising to Baxter. Then again he knew how the IOC handled drug scandals. There was a zero tolerance policy.

The following evening Baxter would sit before a three man IOC Inquiry Commission, chaired by a member of the IOC Juridical Commission, and containing two members of the IOC Medical Commission. It was their job to establish the facts and circumstances of the case. The morning after he would meet with the Disciplinary Commission, comprising five members of the IOC Board. It would be their role to decide if any sanction was to be meted out to Baxter. Their recommendation would be passed to the IOC Executive Board for the final decision.

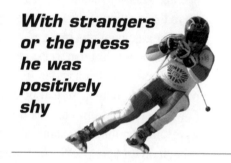

With strangers or the press he was positively shy

Little would be asked of Baxter during the hearings. He would be required to be on hand to answer any questions the Commissions might have and would be given the opportunity to speak in front of both panels should he wish. Friend and Lewis were both keen that Baxter should give his side of the story. Friend wasn't full of confidence after initial attempts to coax the quiet Scotsman out of his shell. He could be gregarious with friends and family but with strangers or the press he was positively shy.

"Adam and I suggested that Alain prepare a statement to read to the Commission. We discussed what he wanted to say to make sure he wouldn't say anything prejudicial but were a little worried because he was reluctant to prepare anything. We crossed our fingers that he wouldn't freeze the following day."

In the early evening of March 15, Baxter and his delegation arrived at the imposing IOC Headquarters in two blacked-out Mercedes-Benz limousines. They felt as if they were attending a Grand Jury mafia trial, and the hordes of waiting press reinforced that feeling. Much to the chagrin of the journalists the convoy of cars drove straight into the IOC's underground car park and away from prying eyes. Everything had gone like clockwork, as planned by the

BOA, but the decision to take the stairwell and not the elevator from the underground car park was less astute – it had glass walls on all sides, affording the perfect opportunity for the paparazzi to capture the final steps of the condemned man.

With Baxter were Clegg, Friend, Lewis, McNeilly, Reedie, Schwaiger, Dickson and Baxter's mother, Sue. They were all fully behind Baxter, even Reedie who, as an IOC member and board member of WADA, was a veritable heavyweight of the Olympic and Anti-Doping movements. They all put on a brave front but harboured deep-seated concerns for their chances of a fair hearing. Friend was still anxious as to whether their arguments would stand up to the scrutiny of the Commission.

"Our argument was very embryonic. We hadn't formulated it beyond that. The hearing was just two weeks after we'd learnt of the failed test. Saying that, if Alain's race had been earlier in the Games we would have been up in front of the IOC in hours. We had been lucky to have time to prepare but deep down we thought our chances were slim. We'd give it our best shot but we were already thinking about the next stage of appeal – the Court of Arbitration for Sport (CAS). We wanted to be one step ahead in case the worst happened."

FACING THE IOC

The IOC Inquiry Commission comprised Denis Oswald (Chairman), Fabio Pigozzi and Yves Larequi. Christa Thiel of WADA was present as an independent observer. The majority of the discourse that evening would be between Oswald and Lewis, who would present Baxter's case. Much of the three hours of legal and scientific debate would go straight over Baxter's head. It felt like being back in school, but he trusted Friend and Lewis to do what was best. They had worked flat-out to put together the case and had recruited a number of respected expert witnesses, whose statements had been submitted prior to the hearing. Dr Bryan Finkle's research formed the scientific cornerstone of the defence.

Lewis opened the proceedings by putting two proposals to the Commission. Firstly, that it adjourn while a simple test be carried out to determine whether the substance in Baxter's sample was the illegal, stimulant form (or D-form) of Methamphetamine or the harmless, medicinal form (or L-form) known as Levmetamfetamine. Despite it not being IOC policy to conduct the Isomer Separation Analysis required, Lewis hoped that the Commission would consider it in light of the threat to Baxter's career. Lewis's second proposal was that, in absence of the test, the Commission find that the IOC had failed to prove that the substance found in Baxter's sample was actually on the banned list. It was a simple proposition, based in science and common sense. Baxter was pleased with Lewis's performance but to him the situation was more simplistic – he had taken something inadvertently but had gained no advantage. A simple test would prove his innocence so he could go back to doing what he loved best. Why should anyone object?

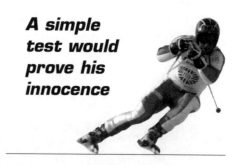

A simple test would prove his innocence

But the Inquiry Commission would object.

Though it didn't question that Baxter had innocently used a Vick's Inhaler, Oswald highlighted in no uncertain terms that the IOC made no distinction between the two forms of Methamphetamine. Rather, that Levmetamfetamine, though not named, came under the umbrella of 'Related Substance' to Methamphetamine in the 'Stimulants' subcategory of its list of prohibited substances. Lewis wasn't surprised by Oswald's response but he fundamentally disagreed with the opinion that the harmless Levmetamfetamine was a related substance of the highly potent street drug Methamphetamine or that it was a powerful stimulant. The document *Doping: An IOC White Paper* laid out the organisation's policy of including unnamed, related substances on its banned list:

> *The rationale for prohibiting related substances is to prevent unscrupulous chemists or persons from promoting new drugs or chemicals that act like prohibited substances but are not specifically named.* (Lausanne 1999, p24)

Baxter's legal team was strongly of the opinion that far from having any stimulant effect, Levmetamfetamine couldn't have acted more differently to its illegal cousin. Lewis told the Commission that it was his belief, and that of his expert witness, that Vick's, which was not a stimulant, that was neither performance-enhancing nor harmful, and that was sold freely over the counter, should not be considered a prohibited substance. The intention of the code, he argued, was never to cover such substances. Where the code referred to Methamphetamine and 'Related Substances', surely it must only apply to the illegal stimulant or designer drugs with similar effects?

The Inquiry Commission appeared unmoved by the argument. Oswald seemed unwilling to enter into any productive debate about the IOC's policies and reminded Baxter and his team that the Commission was there only to establish the facts and circumstances of the case. It was the response Lewis had expected and he used his years of courtroom experience to seize upon Oswald's apparent own goal. Lewis agreed that it was the Commission's role to establish the facts but, he demanded of Oswald, would it not be a key part of that mandate to decide whether Baxter had taken a prohibited substance? Lewis again offered to adjourn should the Commission wish to reassess its position and conduct an ISA test. Lewis felt it was critical that the Disciplinary Commission was provided with the full facts of the case before having to make its decision the following day. Oswald merely acknowledged Lewis's point. There was no attempt to discuss the matter further. The Commission was uncompromising. It did not seem willing even to engage in debate with Baxter's team. To Baxter and his family it smacked of arrogance. Baxter himself was particularly downbeat. It was his livelihood that the Commission was being so blasé about.

SWIMMING AGAINST THE TIDE

"The first hearing was a disaster. It felt as if we were beating our heads against a brick wall. Anything Adam said, the Commission shot down in flames. They seemed to be of the opinion that I'd had a banned substance in my body, it was my fault and I was guilty. As far as I could see they were desperate for me to admit that I was a cheat. They couldn't see, or didn't want to see, what we were telling them. Even though I had the support of Reedie, Clegg, McNeilly, and Schwaiger, a well respected coach and ex-racer, the Commission implied that they were only there because it was Britain's first ever skiing medal."

Despite feeling that he was swimming against the tide, Lewis persevered. He explained why the skier needed to use a Vick's Inhaler and how, earlier in his career, it had been suggested that he have surgery to correct a sinus problem, a fact confirmed by Baxter's GP. Lewis brought to the attention of the Commission that as the packaging of both the UK and US product were virtually identical, that it was perfectly reasonable for him to assume the product he bought in the US was identical to the one he used in Europe.

With his interest piqued, Oswald questioned Baxter directly about events in Salt Lake. He asked the Scot if he'd read the label when he bought the inhaler? (Oswald brought it to the attention of the gathering that L-metamfetamine was listed in the ingredients of the inhaler). Baxter replied that he had not. Assuming he was buying a familiar product, there was no reason to scrutinise the ingredients. Oswald asked why he had not declared his inhaler use to the team doctor or testing centre? Baxter replied that as he'd used the inhaler before it had not even crossed his mind and that after winning the medal he had been excited about fulfilling a childhood dream. Baxter also reminded the Commission that he had not stayed in the Olympic village and had not been in daily contact with team doctors.

Baxter would soon get the chance to elaborate. In the meantime Lewis tried in vain to engage the Commission in productive dialogue. He explained that there was legal precedent concerning 'false positive' drug tests caused by Vick's Inhalers. None of the cases were in sport. It was understood that an athlete looking to cheat would choose something stronger than an over-the-counter medicine and in any case a stimulant would be the last thing a slalom skier would take due to the highly technical nature of the sport. There was no track record of athletes attempting to use it to enhance their performances. There were, Lewis pointed out, a handful of civilian cases in the US where employees had been sacked after testing positive for Methamphatamine in routine tests, only to successfully overturn the decision after proving, via Isomer Separation Analysis, that the banned substance allegedly found was in fact Levmetamfetamine.

Lewis also sought to clarify why the minute trace of 'Methamphetamine' in Baxter's sample had even been flagged in the first place by Dr Don Catlin's IOC-accredited lab at UCLA. Most sports governing bodies in the US used 500 nanograms per ml as the minimum reporting level for Methamphetamine. It hadn't escaped Lewis that the initial fax from the IOC had stated that Baxter's

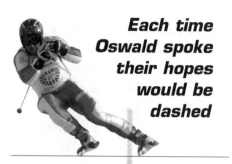

Each time Oswald spoke their hopes would be dashed

sample contained 500 ng/ml of Methamphetamine, only later to be adjusted to 20-25 ng/ml, some 96% lower. Lewis's line of reasoning allowed him to score some valuable points over the IOC. Professor Hemmersbach, a member of the IOC Medical Commission who Oswald called as an expert witness without prior warning, conceded that the IOC did not even require accredited laboratories to have the capability to detect traces of Methamphetamine lower than 500 ng/ml. Baxter could have had twenty times more Levmetamfetamine in his system and most IOC labs around the globe would have been unable, or could decline, to even declare its presence. But the admission seemed to cut no slack with the Commission. It would just be an ironic fact that would drive a less level-headed athlete to distraction in the future.

There were further revelations that, in a sympathetic court, would surely have counted in Baxter's favour. Hemmersbach had reviewed Baxter's positive test result in his role of quality assurance for Salt Lake testing. He had even asked whether Isomer Separation Analysis had been done by the lab after Methamphetamine had been found. Baxter couldn't believe what he was hearing. But, incredulous though it seemed, none of Hemmersbach's colleagues had asked whether they should actually conduct the test after Hemmersbach had mentioned it. Neither had he given them the impression that they should. His reasoning: that it would only have been required if a distinction were made on the IOC list between the different forms of Methamphetamine. The mere fact that Hemmersbach had mentioned the ISA test highlighted that the issue had been discussed before within the corridors of power at the IOC. Hemmersbach admitted that it had, but that he could not recall where or when.

Again, Baxter's team thought they were scoring valid points with the IOC Inquiry Commission. Yet each time Oswald spoke their hopes would be dashed. His highly questionable move of introducing a surprise witness to proceedings, a practice unlikely to have been tolerated by any court in the land, sounded a death knell for Baxter's hopes. Before introducing his star witness Oswald warned Baxter's legal team that he had in his possession evidence that conclusively proved that Levmetamfetamine was a stimulant. It was the phrase they had hoped not to hear. Hemmersbach took the stand to state quite matter of factly that, though it had a different level of activity, there was no doubt that Levmetamfetamine was a stimulant. Even the smallest trace in an athlete's system would be deemed unacceptable. Accurate or not, it was damning evidence.

Lewis countered (after having Hemmersbach confirm that he respected Dr Finkle as a scientist and found him to be reliable) that Finkle had attested that the level of 'Methamphetamine' in Baxter's sample was consistent only with occasional medicinal use of Vick's Inhaler. It was utterly inconceivable that he could have gained any stimulant effect. Again it seemed to cut no ice with the Commission. Even when Hemmersbach admitted that the trace in Baxter's sample did not tally with intentional doping and Lewis noted that it would have taken 80 whole inhalers, melted down, to derive any stimulant effect, the Commission didn't bite. Oswald told Baxter's team that he didn't question whether it was actually Levmetamfetamine that was in his body when he raced or whether he had gained any performance-enhancing or stimulant effect. It only remained for the Commission to decide whether or not it was a prohibited substance. It had made its mind up.

A VERY PERSONAL TESTIMONY

It seems inconceivable that in a country with such stringent medical standards as the United States that Vick's Inhalers would be available over the counter if there were any suspicion whatsoever that they had a stimulant effect. The US is one of the most tightly regulated pharmaceutical markets in the world. It is a country which does not let its young adults drink alcohol until they are 21; and a country which is phobic to class action law suits. It is impossible to link the innocuous Vick's Inhaler sold in every Mom and Pop store across the country with the powerful substance the Inquiry Commission implied was in Baxter's body when he won his medal. There had been a defeated air hanging in the room since Oswald had summoned Hemmersbach and it clung like a fog now. The writing seemed to be on the wall before Baxter had even had the chance to tell his side of the story. He'd prepared nothing but was about to bring a human voice to an inquiry that had seemed unwilling to accept that he'd made an honest mistake. Whether what he would say would make any difference was anybody's guess.

Here is Baxter's recollection of events in Salt Lake:

"The day I arrived in Salt Lake I received a visit from team doctor, Judy Ross. She asked me if I felt okay after the journey. I had my physio with me so I was in good shape. Judy checked my wash-bag. In it I had a couple of herbal sleeping pills that I'd been taking and that was about it. I even gave her the blue dye I'd used to cover the Scottish flag in my hair. Everything was fine. There would usually have been a Vick's Inhaler in my bag but I'd left it at the team base in Lofer. I'd been all over the place the previous two weeks – Aviemore, Italy and Austria – and had forgotten to pack it. I've been using Vick's Inhaler nearly all my life. My sinuses are almost always blocked, they're blocked now, and I've always found Vick's is the best short-term remedy. I could have had an operation to cure my problem but as it would have meant avoiding altitude for several weeks it was never an option.

"Because of the altitude at Salt Lake the air is really dry. The house was warm too. I was jet-lagged and unable to sleep or breathe properly after I arrived. I was sharing a room with my brother and he was blocked-up too. I asked Christian to buy me a Vick's Inhaler like I used at home. He came back with a humidifier for the room and a Vick's Sinex. I told him that I wasn't happy using it because it clears the sinuses too brutally. It's very uncomfortable. I told him, 'That's the wrong product. I'm not even sure if I'm allowed to take it.' So we got it checked by the team doctor and it was fine. I still found it was too harsh so used it only once.

"Later that week I had a bad training crash. My physio offered me Ibuprofen, but I didn't even want to take it until we'd checked it with Judy. Eventually I took just one, even though my back and knee hurt for days. After the crash I took a couple of days off. When the others were skiing I went into Park City to visit the shops. I bought some juice, some muesli bars, some more videos and saw a Vick's Inhaler. I grabbed it so I wouldn't have to use the Vick's Sinex again. It was the same brand, the same product, virtually identical packaging with the same logo and colours as the one I used in Europe. When I got back to the house my sinuses where blocked so I used it. The days I did need it I'd use the inhaler no more than three times a day.

"It hadn't occurred to me to check the inhaler with the doctor. I knew that it was clear in Europe and there was nothing to suggest that it was a different product. There was a list of products like Lemsip and Benylin that I knew were banned as we'd received leaflets about it from the BOA. If I'd needed to use something like that or another decongestant product I would have been suspicious and asked the doctor before using it.

I bought the wrong inhaler but that's all

"After winning the bronze I went to the doping centre to give a sample. I had to declare anything I'd been taking. I think I put the herbal sleeping pills down but I knew I hadn't been taking anything else. The inhaler didn't even cross my mind. It was a bit of a blur to tell you the truth because I was so excited by what had just happened."

Baxter paused for a moment and made eye contact with the panel for the first time.

"I don't see what I've done wrong? I made an honest mistake. I bought the wrong inhaler but that's all. Can't you see that?"

Friend was taken aback by Baxter's testimony. It couldn't have been more compelling.

"We didn't know what to expect from Alain. He was so softly spoken and he didn't look comfortable in a shirt and tie, let alone a courtroom but he came across as being incredibly genuine. You couldn't fail to be moved by it. When he spoke it was clear to everyone that he wasn't acting or lying. He didn't have it in him."

It was a heartfelt plea. Though certain members of the Commission would later admit, off the record, that they felt huge sympathy for Baxter, they would have their hands tied. Rules were rules. No matter how unfortunate, Baxter had won a medal with a banned substance in his body – that would be their recommendation to the Disciplinary Committee. McNeilly remembers that the mood in Baxter's camp was particularly low after the hearing.

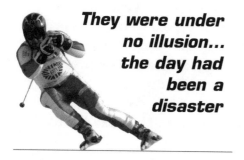

They were under no illusion... the day had been a disaster

"The first hearing was an absolute low point. I didn't feel we were going to get justice there. I didn't get the impression that the Medical Commission was there to even consider that there might be flaws in its own rules. We were all very low. There was no cause for hope."

Baxter and his team dejectedly filtered out of the room. They were all under no illusion that the day had been a disaster. As they made their way to the underground car park something extraordinary happened. According to several eyewitnesses, Schwaiger recognised some Austrian skiers entering the IOC Headquarters. It was not an everyday occurrence for athletes to be summoned by the IOC, unless of-course they had a case to answer. The IOC had only announced that five athletes at Salt Lake had failed drugs tests – Baxter, a Belarusian ice hockey player and three cross-country skiers – though rumours were rife that the cross country team from one of the big Alpine nations was caught up in a doping scandal. Baxter had too much on his mind to consider why the other athletes might have been there. They certainly weren't alpine skiers or he would have recognised them too. And besides, the sport just didn't have a culture of cheating. There was no drug *de jour* in the sport. Cycling has EPO, sprinting has Nandrolone. If there was a drug to improve slalom performance no-one had ever told Baxter about it.

The alleged sighting raised a question that had been on many people's lips. How would Baxter's case have been treated if he had been an American or an Austrian skier? Would the procedure have been different if he was from one of the bigger countries which helped bankroll the International Ski Federation? Was he deemed an easy target because he'd been caught up in a political scandal over the Saltire sprayed in his hair? Did the IOC feel under pressure after numerous incidents in its own back yard, such as the Salt Lake bidding scandal, when IOC members traded votes for cash, and the high profile Ice Skating judging scandal, where a French judge was pressured into marking a Russian couple higher than their more deserving Canadian counterparts in the pairs. Did they want to make an example of someone to re-establish their hard-line on sleaze? The IOC didn't have such a snow-white reputation at the time. There was a well-documented case of a Norwegian athlete's sample being dropped in a lab by a Norwegian IOC scientist. In his book, *Inside the Olympics*, former IOC Vice President, Dick Pound, even states that as an organisation it had its back against the wall after Salt Lake: 'The IOC itself had failed to live up to the ethical expectations it had created for the Olympic movement.' Was Baxter the right athlete, in the wrong place at the wrong time?

These were arguments for another lifetime, as far as Baxter was concerned. He didn't entertain any talk of conspiracy theories. His focus was on the Disciplinary Commission the following day. He prayed that it would acknowledge his innocent mistake and show him some lenience.

That evening, Baxter called his father for the first time since he'd fled Aviemore. Ian Baxter reassured his son that justice would be done and his son went to sleep more optimistic than Lewis or Friend. The Disciplinary Commission commenced at 11am the following morning. The panel comprised Thomas Bach (Chairman), Gunilla Lindberg, Sergei Bubka (ex-pole vaulter and a man tipped as a future president of the IOC), Lambis Nikolaou and Toni Khoury. Christa Thiel of WADA was the independent observer and the IOC's Director General, François Carrard, and Director of Legal Affairs, Howard Stupp, also sat in.

The second part of Baxter's hearing was considerably briefer than the first. It lasted just 55 minutes, during which time Lewis summarised events from the day before. He reiterated his request for the ISA test to be carried out and the Disciplinary Commission responded that it would be a decision for the IOC Executive Board to take. Lewis highlighted Baxter's 'consistently good character', and urged that to be stripped of his medal would be a very serious consequence for someone who had clearly not cheated. Baxter was given a chance to give his version of events and made an impassioned plea for justice. He admitted, rather humbly, that he had 'simply made a mistake'. Reedie brought proceedings to a close by highlighting that the case rested on a completely inflexible rule in the Olympic Movement Anti-Doping Code, reminding the Commission that it was their role to protect athletes. As both delegations began to file out Baxter was approached by Bubka and another member of the Commission.

"The second day gave me hope. I'd told them exactly what had happened and they listened. It helped having Bubka, who was an ex-athlete, on the board. After the hearing he asked if he could see the UK and US inhalers. He looked at the US inhaler and said, 'I think I've actually taken that one before'. It gave me some encouragement that finally someone was seeing my side of the story and might actually fight my corner."

Having taken place after official proceedings Baxter's conversation with Bubka was not recorded in transcripts of the hearing but McNeilly recalls seeing the two locked in discussion for some time.

"I saw Alain and Bubka deep in conversation after the hearing. I don't know what they said but they were looking at the inhalers and Alain clearly drew a lot of hope from speaking with him."

AWAITING THE VERDICT

Baxter and McNeilly would drive back to London together that day. It was the only way to escape the overbearing gaze of the media. Baxter would not make a statement until the IOC delivered its verdict. Baxter returned to Moulder-

The Fight Begins

Brown's family home in Chelsea where he resumed the routine of training, watching television, eating and sleeping. He'd been told by Clegg that the IOC could take up to a week to come to a decision but that they would be given 30 hours notice of the IOC announcement to enable them to release their own statement first. Clegg told Baxter to sit tight, stay indoors and not speak to the press.

Baxter soon got bored with being under house arrest. It had been better in Norway where he could at least ski and walk the streets. But he was back in London where he had friends and was getting itchy feet. He and Moulder-Brown, who'd had a reputation as the team's resident telly addicts in the past, watched film after film. It was only after watching a whole series of *Friends* back-to-back that Baxter snapped. He called Dan and Roger Walker, Mark Riley and Adam Sullivan, some of whom he hadn't seen in years. They met in Camden and strolled around the market. It took Baxter's mind off waiting and after stopping at a pub the group soon got talking about old times. It was a great release for Baxter, having not known a normal life for weeks. By early evening Baxter eyed his watch. Clegg had said they'd get 30

The IOC had gone back on its word

hours notice. If they hadn't been told by now there would be no way he'd have to do a press conference the following day – it was decided: they'd make a night of it, and Baxter's problems seemed to fade with every drink.

"It was a great night. I really needed it after being cooped up for so long. I finally got to bed at 4am but I'm not the best sleeper so I was awake again after a couple of hours. I went downstairs and put *The Matrix* video on. I switched my phone on and it rang within minutes. I thought it might have been a voice message but it was Fiona. She said she was coming in an hour to take me to the BOA offices. The IOC decision was imminent and they were going to make an official announcement later that morning. I said: 'What happened to 30 hours? I was drunk last night. Do I have any choice?'"

Baxter had no choice. The IOC had gone back on its word, giving the BOA just three hours to prepare for its official release. It would jeopardise the good relations McNeilly had forged with the press, especially in Scotland, who she'd promised 24 hours notice of any press conference. Now they'd get just two. The BOA had planned one press conference in central London that morning and McNeilly hastily arranged a second at The Cairngorm Hotel, the scene of Baxter's glorious homecoming, the following day. Dare they dream of a second triumphant return?

Baxter showered and dressed, not even having time to shave. At the BOA office Baxter, Clegg and McNeilly waited anxiously for news from the IOC. Time seemed to slow. Minutes seemed to take hours to pass but finally the fax machine sparked into life. Baxter felt a knot tighten in his stomach. Combined with his hangover it made him feel nauseous.

"Simon read through the fax carefully and looked up. 'Sorry Alain,' was all he said. I couldn't believe it. I was gutted. I didn't even think about the medal or having the result erased from the record books. I was thinking more about how long my ban was going to be. It opened a whole new can of worms."

It was March 21, 2002. 26 days after Baxter had stood proudly on the Olympic podium. He'd only been able to bask in the glory for five days before the IOC had pulled the rug from under him. At the press conference Reedie conveyed the IOC ruling to the media: Baxter had been disqualified from the Men's Slalom at Salt Lake and would be stripped of his medal; FIS had wiped the result from its records, made the relevant deductions to Baxter's world ranking and would issue a ban in due course. Reedie softened the blow by adding, unprompted that, "Alain could not be considered a drugs cheat. His offence was modest but the penalty severe."

THE SUPPORT BUILDS

It was the first time Baxter had faced the British press since the homecoming. He desperately wanted to tell his story but was fazed by the incessant questions and shouting. It was a free-for-all. Seeing he was flummoxed, Philip Pope brought the press conference to a premature end and scheduled less intimidating one-to-one interviews. Baxter did live interviews for BBC, ITN, Channel 4, Sky Sports, not to mention numerous newspapers. Again, the majority of the press coverage would be supportive. He posed for pictures with the two inhalers and *The Daily Record* ran with it on the front page, manipulating the image, turning the two inhalers into a big V sign directed at the IOC. It was a message from all its readers to the IOC. As much two fingers up to the powers that be as two thumbs up for Baxter. He had their full backing.

Baxter was whisked off from the conference to be Nicky Campbell's guest on his BBC Five Live phone-in. The majority of callers were supportive but Baxter was taken aback by some of the vitriolic abuse he had to suffer.

"One caller said, 'You cheated, didn't you?' It took me by surprise and really wound me up. I tried to control myself. I asked him if he'd listened to a word I'd said. He went on, 'Everyone says that. Everyone says they didn't cheat. Why don't you just admit you had a couple of blasts of speed before the race.' I was stuck for words. The next caller said his name but I was sure I recognised the voice. He said, 'That guy who called before was a complete arsehole. He should think about what he's saying. I believe you and so does most of the country.' As soon as I got out of the studio Roger Walker, who I'd been out with the night before, called up. It had been him."

For Baxter it was the same as when he had won the medal. In those first hours he never had a solitary moment for the news to sink in. In hindsight, it was probably a good thing. He faced the world's press in a daze but somehow managed to get through it. Travelling up to Aviemore the next day, events of the previous three weeks began to take their toll. He could have been finished. It was as simple as that. A two year ban from FIS was not out of the question. The pressure leading up to the inquiry would have ripped most people apart, let alone the decision to strip him of his medal. That Baxter had got this far before succumbing to his emotions was nothing short of miraculous. It had demanded super-human self control. Only Baxter can explain how it felt to finally return home after what he'd been through.

"When I drove into Aviemore for the press conference it was unbelievable. It was the most emotional time of my whole Olympic experience. To see how much support I had there was amazing. There were cars going round with stickers saying, 'Support Baxter' and 'Baxter is Innocent.' People were beeping their horns as I drove by. Someone had made an 8ft tall bronze medal and hung it from a crane for me to see as soon as I got back to the village.

"When we pulled up to the hotel it was like the homecoming all over again. Hundreds of people were there cheering, clapping. A young girl ducked under a security barrier and ran up to the car. It was the little girl who'd hugged my leg at the primary school and she presented me with a homemade bronze medal. I had a lump in my throat. It was all I could do to hold back my emotions. I didn't know what to think. I had never expected this. I was hurting inside but the attitude of people there was so fantastic. It was so hard for me to express how that felt. How much it meant coming from them. I couldn't put it into words.

"That was the hardest press conference of all, the hardest thing I've ever had to do, in front of the people that knew me best. I almost broke down but somehow I got through it. I composed myself and tried to explain to everyone what had happened but I'd catch a glimpse of my family in the front row, my mates in the back row, and I'd have to stop. The lump in my throat would well up again. I was completely choked. It was unbelievable. That was the end of a three and half week journey that I'll never forget. I had been as high and as low as it's possible for anyone to be."

> CHAPTER 6   **UP THE RANKINGS**

SEASON 1996/1997
SEASON 1997/1998
SEASON 1998/1999
SEASON 1999/2000

6   UP THE RANKINGS

Baxter's ultimatum to the BSSF for a new coach wasn't the bolt out the blue that it might have been. Chief Executive, Mike Jardine, was already putting final plans in place to revolutionise how the team was run. What little resources the Federation had would be devoted to quality coaching for its elite skiers. Were he to return, Baxter would be welcomed back with open arms. Others would not be so lucky, falling victim to deliberately high qualification standards.

After missing the training camp it didn't take Baxter long to get itchy feet. He hadn't skied for months and started to miss it. The previous season had been awful, but he had come to realise that he did not want to end his career on such a low note. Deep down he knew that he could do better. The seemingly endless black cloud which had engulfed the easy-going Scot was beginning to disappear.

"After I missed the camp my conscience kicked in. I started to think that I hadn't given it my best shot. Maybe I needed to stick it out a little longer. People have always criticised British skiers for not persevering, for quitting when things got tough, but sometimes you have to be patient. I knew I wasn't going to make an immediate impact at international level. You've got to go through the ups and downs to get to the other side."

It was an important realisation. Baxter was finally thinking straight. But it took the appointment of Austrian ex-World Cup racer Mathias Berthold as coach to move Baxter to sign up for the season. It would prove a shrewd decision.

"I clicked with Mathias straightaway. We were pretty similar people. He'd just finished racing and he had a lot of good advice to give me, much like Colin Grant when I was younger. Mathias was fresh and excited about coaching us.

"He came in, saw I had a bit of talent and went 'OK, lets see what we can do with this.' When I joined up with the team there was a lot of work to be done. But I'd been training at home and I was feeling good. What was totally new to me was that Mathias would train on the course with us. He'd say, 'Come on guys, follow me,' and fly off down the piste. It was tough to keep up. It was just what I needed at that time."

For Matthias it was his first job as a coach:

"When I first started working for the British Ski Federation, the Head Coach at the time told me that I should have a look at the team and decide who I wanted to work with. He told me about Alain Baxter, saying that he was a 'very difficult guy', and if I didn't want to work with him it would fine by the Ski Federation. Well I met Alain, and the 'difficult guy' seemed to me to be a really nice guy. We had a perfect working relationship right from the start, and my first impression was that he had everything one needs to become one of the world's best skiers.

"I don't know if he was underperforming before we started working together. I just tried to teach him everything that I knew, and tried to pass on all the experience that I'd had over the years.

The 'difficult guy' seemed to me to be a really nice guy

"We did a lot of ski technique training from the very beginning, lots of technique drills and exercises. We only started race training after I felt that he was at the right technical level. Another thing we worked on was a mental game plan, because he used to have a very strong and high temper which wasn't always helpful for the progress of training. His reaction to all these new things was very good. Of course it took a while before he trusted me but after that it was just perfect to work with him.

"I think it was probably the first time that someone told him that he could really make it all the way to the top, which at first he didn't really believe, but after a while when he saw how fast he was improving in the world rankings he started to realise that he might have a chance."

SEASON: 1996/97

Age: 22/23
World Ranking: 438

Baxter's unstinting demand for better coaching would mark the turnaround for the British team. Berthold had been a successful racer and had an abundance of wisdom to pass on. From wanting to quit just one month before, Baxter soon found himself living in Gargellen, Austria, with young team-mates Jonny Moulder-Brown and Ross Green. The Federation's cutbacks had been sweeping. That would be as much of a team as Baxter would know for the next four years.

Baxter took to Gargellen immediately. It was not unlike Aviemore. It felt like home and he soon made friends in the village. He was feeling altogether more settled and was a different person from the previous season. Life was good, both on and off the piste.

Berthold had raised the bar in training and Baxter had responded. He trained hard and by November was ready to race. Baxter's season-opener was in a FIS Race in Hochgurgl, Austria. He finished a respectable 27th (GS).

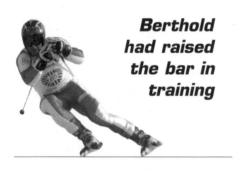

Berthold had raised the bar in training

Berthold's experience was already coming to the fore, however, and for the first time Baxter would spend December racing largely on the Nor-Am Cup tour in the US. Baxter's ranking was so poor that it was imperative he regained ground as quickly as possible. FIS did seven ranking lists per year so if Baxter performed well in the Nor-Ams he could improve his start position as early as January. The Nor-Am tour was thought to be the perfect place to gain ranking points. Unlike Europe, races there were contested by fewer skiers, thus Baxter's chances of a better result were higher. Baxter's results would be mixed, however. Despite coming 2nd (GS) in a FIS Race in Vermont and 14th (GS) in a Nor-Am Cup in Sunday River, Maine, Baxter failed to finish the final two races of the trip. It was deemed a success, nevertheless, as Baxter had scored valuable ranking points in the first two races.

Berthold had complete faith in his top skier, regardless of the odd crash. Straddling was an integral part of Slalom and GS. It was unavoidable in such a risk/reward sport. Berthold instilled a confidence in Baxter that he'd so far lacked. The Austrian saw a little of himself in the Scot. The two shared a love of fast cars and a do-or-die attitude which lent itself well to racing. There was a mutual respect. As so often in his career, when confronted with someone who had achieved so much, far from feeling threatened, Baxter showed a willingness to listen and learn. He looked up to Berthold and thought, 'You've been there and done it and I can too.'

Never one to tread the path of least resistance, Baxter returned to racing in January only to crash out of his first two races. But Berthold spurred him on. He'd seen what Baxter was capable of in training and he wanted to see it in races.

"Watching him skiing in training he seems to be the very best slalom skier in the world, it

Alain in training

is just extremly difficult for him to perform at the same level in the races. Austrians have to perform in almost every training session as if it were a race otherwise they would not get to race. But being from Scotland there is no real competition in training. No-one else is performing at the same level, and so you are always the best until you start at a World Cup, then it is really difficult to step up and ski at the highest level all of a sudden. It's just a lot more difficult than if you are part of a big programme like the one in Austria, though it is also very hard being part of the Austrian team because athletes have to perform at the highest level from a very young age or they will get eliminated at a very young age. It is difficult to say if Alain would have done better or worse if he had come from a big skiing country. Alain is one of the best athletes and one of the best skiers that I know and it is painful for me that he lost his Olympic medal. He deserved it so much."

Baxter's persistence, and Berthold's faith, were paid off in spade-fulls from

this point on. Baxter was back in the groove and, crucially, was confident. In a whirlwind five weeks up to the World Ski Championships in mid-February, Baxter posted the following results (FIS Races, unless stated): 20th (Slalom), 38th, 28th, 32nd, 24th, 28th (GS), DNF1, 30th (Super G), 10th, 5th (Slalom, Germany National Junior Championships) and 8th (GS). There was a trend of improvement and Baxter was in good shape for his second World Championships, in Sestriere. Yet he straddled on his first run and that was that. Berthold didn't let Baxter dwell on it. His world ranking was moving in the right direction and one bad result wasn't worth losing sleep over.

Baxter attacked the remaining races that season with relish. He could only manage 6th place in the GS at the British Championships and straddled in the Slalom but he'd learnt the lesson the year before that in the bigger picture being British Champion meant little. Baxter returned to North America alone in March. Coach-less, Baxter trained in Canada with local skiers. While there he opportunistically entered a Dual Slalom – where two racers go head-to-head on adjacent, identical courses in a knockout competition. It suited Baxter's aggressive style and competitive nature and he won the experimental format and the $1,000 winner's cheque. It was the first money Baxter had won in seven years of full-time racing. Flush with success, Baxter did some Tax Free shopping before his next race in Mont Tremblant, Quebec. There, he entered a GS, Super G and a Slalom, finishing 29th, 65th, and straddling in the latter.

Happy with his technique and form, Baxter was conversely growing increasingly disillusioned with his equipment. He'd been around long enough to know that a good performance comprised many variables. There was technique, physical condition, mental condition, weather conditions, start position and equipment. Baxter had been on Kastle skis for three years but felt that he was struggling to turn them – a critical misgiving for the multiple tight, fast turns demanded by the sport. Baxter was still not getting paid to wear a particular brand of ski and so he was happy to experiment.

"After Canada, I moved to Sunday River for a couple of FIS Races. I wasn't happy with my skis at all. I met a young British skier who was studying there and asked if I could borrow his training skis. He was on Rossignol. I did the first run on Kastle and was 7th fastest. For the next run I put on the Rossignols and came down into 1st. It was my best result of the season by far. After that I said, 'You've got to let me borrow those skis for the rest of my trip'."

Baxter was granted his wish and went on to score the best results of his career on a pair of borrowed skis. He followed up his 1st place with a repeat result the following day. From there he finished the season in impressive style. Aside from inevitably straddling in one race, Baxter finished 7th, 5th, 12th, 8th, 6th, 5th and 2nd in consecutive FIS Races. He was scoring consistent top ten finishes and it gave his ranking the shot in the arm it needed. It went without saying that Baxter switched to Rossignols the following season.

There had been false dawns before but Baxter finally felt that he was starting to ski near his full potential. No longer was he leaving his best performances on the training slopes. Baxter's Slalom ranking climbed over 150 places to 289. He was back in business and didn't want the season to end. But he needn't have worried. Berthold had ushered in a new era of professionalism. He would have Baxter racing in the Southern Hemisphere before he knew it. Whether he'd build on the impressive end to the season in North America was anyone's guess. But what was guaranteed was that he'd laid some formidable foundations from which to launch an assault on the top 100.

SEASON: 1997/98

Age: 23/24
World Ranking: 289

Baxter received a massive funding boost in 1997 when the National Lottery began funding skiing as part of a larger initiative in sport. He received £3,000 per year in training expenses. As it was an Olympics season, Baxter was eligible for the Talented Athlete Programme. It was a god-send. The Lottery funding was the boost that the sport needed, though Baxter still had to work in the summer, landing another gardening job.

The BSSF continued to be true to its word to focus on its elite athletes. Realising that Baxter would be a one man band that season – Moulder-Brown and Green attended lower ranking events – it made enquiries with the Swiss and Canadian teams to see if Baxter could train with them for a season. It is commonplace for small nations to palm their skiers off onto bigger teams and is a mutually beneficial arrangement. The skier gains a team, while the team gain an extra coach or any support staff the skier brings. Both teams were happy for Baxter to join but wanted the Scot to pay £20,000 for the season. This was on top of the £20,000 it was already costing. He was keen but his sponsor, the Aviemore Brewery, couldn't stretch to the extra expense. Baxter and Berthold were on their own.

That summer, the senior and junior teams went to Porter Heights, New Zealand, to train. It made the Alps look technologically sophisticated. The chalet that the teams shared had no mains electricity, only a generator that switched itself off at 10pm. A ski team has probably never sustained so many minor toe and foot injuries, as they continually bumped into doors and walls after lights out. At the camp, Baxter would meet his future coach Christian Schwaiger, who was coaching the juniors. He didn't know it but this would be his last season with Berthold.

Baxter was put through his paces for three weeks. The Japanese team trained nearby too, so it was another new experience to see their methods and meet their top racers. Baxter found it a stimulating environment. In August, the team travelled to Coronet Peak to race. It couldn't have come soon enough. Baxter was eager to take up from where he'd left off the season before.

In the four FIS Races he came 3rd, 2nd (GS), 2nd and 4th (Slalom). Come the start of the Northern Hemisphere season he had reduced his ranking further to 211 and was about to sample World Cup racing for the first time.

It was a major milestone to finally compete on the World Cup circuit. It was what he'd dreamed of since watching his heroes Marco Girardelli and Ingemar Stenmark on *Ski Sunday* as a child. Baxter had long-since achieved the minimum standard to qualify for Britain's one allocated place on the World Cup start line but it was only now that Berthold felt he was ready to compete at the highest level. Baxter's world ranking was such that it was still too high to enable him to make any real impact in the races, however. He was there to gain experience and perhaps turn some heads by being fastest over the occasional split (courses are divided into sections, where skier's split times are instantaneously displayed enabling commentators to compare skiers as they race).

It sucked. I wanted to be up there with them

In World Cup races the top 75 skiers in the world start according to their ranking, with the exception of the top 15 whose order is decided by a draw (of start numbers 1-15) before the race. Start number is everything in skiing. The better ranked skiers tackle the course first, when it is pristine, while the tail-enders are left to dodge the ruts later on. Only the 30 fastest skiers qualify for the second of the two runs, racing in reverse order, with the fastest last. Starting well down the field, Baxter would have caused a sensation to even make the second run but, in his debut in Tignes, he finished well outside the top 30. By this stage Berthold had managed to strike a deal with the German Team for Baxter to train with them in Europe in October and in the US in November. Baxter remembers it as being a significant step up from what he'd been used to.

"The standard with the Germans was high. The older guys in their team didn't know me and assumed that I was ranked about 40 because I was training with them and putting in a good account of myself. I was actually ranked around 200 but was skiing really well. I'd often beat the better-ranked guys in training but when it came to races I started 70 places down the field from the same guys and could get nowhere near them. It sucked. I wanted to be up there with them. I said to myself, 'Okay, it's time to start doing this in races'."

After Tignes, Baxter and Berthold travelled to Park City with the Germans. Baxter did fitness training alone, ski training with the team, and would eat alone or with Berthold. He didn't mind the solitude. He'd joined the team to learn, not socialise. Buoyed by his improving performances in training Baxter eagerly anticipated his second World Cup.

"I couldn't wait to get started at Park City. I battered out of the start gate in the GS. I was in the tuck, pushing over the rolls, picking up more speed. At the top it was really flat then there was a really steep pitch. I skied as hard as I could and ended up 31st from a starting position of about 70. I'd just missed out on qualifying for the second run but was getting closer. I got the 5th best time on the top split and my performance was commented on by a lot of the other skiers. To make up 40 places was a great result for anyone."

Baxter entered the World Cup Slalom but missed the cut too (eventually the event would be his sole focus but Berthold thought it beneficial to his development to still race in GS). He was going to have to bring down his start number if he was ever going to qualify for a second run. And this is how Baxter would spend much of his season up until the Nagano Winter Olympics in February. He'd only do two more World Cups (qualifying for the second run in neither) and instead concentrated on winning ranking points in second tier races. Highlights of that pre-Olympic period included 12 top ten finishes – including two victories, a 2nd and a 3rd place – out of 28 starts. Baxter went to Nagano full of hope.

"The Olympics looked promising. I was excited because it was my first Games but my race was two hours from Nagano so I stayed nearby, away from all the diversions of the village. It was the first year that they'd injected the piste with water. It was bullet-proof, which helped people like me starting further back. It was also the first time they'd used a rope to set the course so everything was symmetrical, which seemed to agree with me.

"I started 119th in the Slalom. I skied well and was 10th fastest in the final split when I hooked a gate and crashed. I had been ahead of Alberto Tomba! I couldn't believe it. It was frustrating to have crashed, but it was nice to see that I could ski that fast. It felt like I'd made a big breakthrough in the Slalom."

Baxter finished 31st in the GS which was impressive given his start number of 191. He'd beaten 160 better ranked skiers. He had a taste for Olympic competition and couldn't wait until Salt Lake four years later when he'd hope to be in a better position. But he'd fulfilled one of his childhood dreams by competing there. In the early days, writing sponsorship portfolios with his mother, it would be the first thing he'd put on the page when outlining his aspirations. The ambitious child

would never have dared share his real dream. That wasn't just to compete at the Olympics, Baxter wanted more than anything to win a medal.

Baxter used the Olympic experience as a springboard for further success. His final 16 races of the season garnered 10 top ten finishes, including four podiums. Baxter was eating into his ranking and ended the gruelling season ranked 87th. He had reached the promised land of the top 100. It felt light years away from just two years earlier when he had considered quitting. The top 100 meant a lot of things, aside from the prestige. It also opened the door to extra funding from Sport Scotland via The National Lottery. To claim this funding Baxter would have to pay a little more attention to his book-keeping. It was a cause of some frustration for BSSF Alpine Secretary, Fiona McNeilly.

"Athletes had to file quarterly expense claims but by the third quarter Alain had done nothing. He is not a receipt gatherer. He could not face the paperwork, though he really needed the money. At this stage I would reluctantly go through this indecipherable pile of confetti and try and figure out what had been spent where. I'm not sure that it was good for him but I knew that if I didn't do it, he never would."

It would be wrong to judge Baxter without putting it into context. So focused was Baxter on being a success, that money took a back seat. Everything took a back seat, including relationships and family engagements.

As when he'd bounced Eurocheques around Europe as a teenager, Baxter only cared about making it to the next race and posting a decent result. Funding was something to worry about in the off-season. Baxter would soon buck up his ideas, however. The notion that he might one day make a living from the sport was not as distant as it had once been.

SEASON: 1998/99

Age: 24/25
World Ranking: 87

Despite the quantum leap in funding, Baxter was still required to take a summer job in 1998 and worked with Cammy Munro putting in miles and miles of fencing around the Cairngorm National Park. It was a gruelling job but, despite being one of the world's top skiers, there were no airs and graces about Baxter. He had one of his best summers in memory. The physical demands of fencing were adding extra muscle to his frame which could only help to improve his performance on skis and, when he wasn't working, he'd train, play ice hockey, golf, shinty, tennis or sleep. It was a packed summer.

Baxter moved out of his mother's house that summer too. He'd been reunited with a childhood sweetheart and started a relationship. Donna Orr shared a house with Baxter's friend Stork and soon after he moved in too. The three shared a small cottage, christened 'The Beach House' despite being in the heart of the land-locked Spey Valley. It was run-down and poky but Baxter liked it. He was enjoying the things he had missed out on through skiing, such as living with friends and having a normal relationship. The season-start would put paid to Baxter's summer of love, however, and Orr would move to New Zealand and marry within months.

At the end of the previous season Berthold had accepted an offer to coach the Austrian national team. It was too good to refuse. He'd enjoyed his time with Baxter and had taken particular pride from seeing him come of age as a skier. He couldn't help feeling that there was more to come from the Scot. In place of Berthold came Christian Schwaiger, another ex-Austrian racer. Schwaiger was a different character to Berthold altogether but hit it off with

Baxter immediately. Baxter would essentially be a one man team again in the 98/99 season. When he had first joined the team there had been six skiers above him and the same number coming through from the junior team. Now he was the last man standing from those days, excepting Moulder-Brown and Green, who would not catch up with Baxter for a couple of seasons. This wasn't necessarily a disadvantage. Having found his informal training arrangement with the German team extremely rewarding the year before, Schwaiger arranged for Baxter to train with the talented Finnish team during the season. The team contained two rising stars of the Slalom world, Kalle Palander and Mika Marila, and Baxter made the most of the opportunity to train day in, day out with them.

Baxter started his season at a World Cup race in Sölden, Austria. As in the season before, Baxter would battle but would not make it into the top 30. He'd still to qualify for a second World Cup run and it became an obsession. Baxter was learning with every race, however, and by early January had raced in nine World Cups, significantly more than he'd done in the previous season. But he was still starting too far down the field to make an impact. Baxter was getting a taste for podium finishes in second tier races, meanwhile, and was getting noticed as a result. His profile was growing. He was doing so many races by this time that the season would pass in a blur, punctuated only by World Cup races and by the World Championships in Vail. It would be Baxter's third Championships and going into the February 1999 event on the back of two top ten finishes at the Austrian Nationals, he hoped he could improve on his result at the previous World Championships.

"I really wanted to be finishing in the teens that year. Palander and Marila were both doing well that season so training was good. They were pushing me to a higher level."

21-year-old Palander would win the World Championships. Baxter would be happy with his 22nd place in the Slalom and 28th in the GS. He was punching above his weight, finishing over 60 places above his ranking in both events, and he took particular pride in beating former-Olympic champion Finn Christian Jagge in the Slalom.

Baxter was skiing on Rossignol skis that season. The tools of his trade measured 198cm. Yet toward the end of the season the Scot started noticing that some skiers had begun to experiment with skis as short as 170cm. For someone who had amassed an encyclopaedic knowledge of skis from his years of preparing his own equipment, it was intriguing. What intrigued him even more, though, was that the skiers racing on the shorter skis were starting to win races. In late March, Baxter finished 4th in a Slalom in Austria. The race was won by someone on short skis and it was all Baxter could do to tear his eyes away from the winner's skis.

"Mitja Valencic won and made it look so easy. I bumped into my ex-coach Mathias who said, 'You've got to get a pair, these are perfect for you.' He made a call and there was a pair waiting for me where we trained. I mounted up the skis. They were tiny, about 170cm, and I went freeskiing with them. I remember carving with them, and getting so much acceleration. I had a shot on the Slalom course and it felt so easy. Everything was coming at me so quickly. When I went back on normal skis I was a second and half slower. I couldn't wait to race with the new skis."

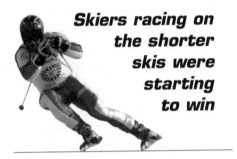

Skiers racing on the shorter skis were starting to win

After only four proper runs on the revolutionary skis, Baxter went to the German Championships in Seefeld. He started 14th and was leading by over half a second after the first run. Baxter was stunned. 'This is more like it!' he thought to himself. He finished 2nd overall and never skied on long skis again. It was another pivotal moment for the Scot. Throughout his career he had always reacted well to change. When he trained with better skiers, invariably he improved dramatically. When race organisers started injecting pistes with water for a more durable surface it marked the start of Baxter's rise through the rankings. Now Baxter seemed to immediately adapt to the new carving skis. Baxter couldn't say why he took to them better than some of his peers. Some said it suited his aggressive style, others that his talent for ice-skating prediposed him to the shorter skis. All that Baxter cared about was that they made him ski faster.

By the time Baxter arrived in Sunday River in early April for the first in a series of FIS Races, most of the other racers were on short skis too. But Baxter won the two Slalom races, going on to win two of his next eight races, and coming 3rd in another. It was a positive way to end the season. On paper 1998/99 was a year of consolidation. Baxter hadn't wanted to crash into the top 100 only to slide straight back out again. A balance was required between chasing the holy grail of the World Cup tour, where he'd yet to win a ranking point, and plugging away at second tier events to maintain or reduce his world ranking. Baxter ended the season ranked 105th for Slalom. He had slipped slightly from the year before but would soon bounce back. It hadn't felt like a breakthrough year as the season before had, but Baxter felt comfortable to be gaining experience in the top flight. As in the previous two seasons, Baxter couldn't bear to see the season end. For the first time in his career he actually felt that he had an advantage over some of his fellow skiers. He hoped that his slight edge would not be eroded over the summer.

SEASON: 1999/2000

Age: 25/26
World Ranking: 105

In the summer of 1999 Baxter worked again with Cammy Munro. The hard graft gave him a powerful physique. All the hours in the gym couldn't match raising a 20kg hammer into the air repeatedly to knock in fence posts all day. The work paid for Baxter's at-home expenses too, which was doubly valuable. But now Baxter faced a serious funding gap, having recently seen a principal sponsor withdraw. He was thousands of pounds short for the coming season before picking up a new sponsor in the knick of time. Scott Oswald Accountants put up a considerable amount of money to support Baxter and got him out of a bind that could have thwarted his dream at the final hurdle.

He was relieved to see that he was skiing as fast as anyone on the new skis during summer training. Some of the other racers appeared to be having problems adapting to the new equipment and it gave Baxter renewed hope that this could be the season he'd really make a name for himself. Nothing seemed to come easy for the Scot, however.

"I was really excited because the sport had made a great leap forward. But

I had to start the season skiing on off-the-shelf skis, not Factory skis like everyone else. Rossignol had made 170cm and 177cm Factory models the season before. The majority of the skiers liked the 177, apart from me, because it didn't have as much of a sidecut as the 170. This meant you didn't get as much kickback from them, or as much speed. Because I was the only one using the 170 it was discontinued. I had to start using the bog-standard production ski, but because they weren't built for racing they broke really easily."

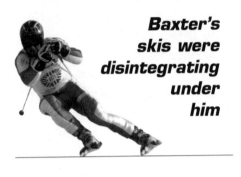

Baxter's skis were disintegrating under him

Baxter went to the first World Cup in Tignes with the skis and was not altogether surprised to crash out on the first run. From there, he headed to the US and raced in a Nor-Am Cup in Breckenridge. Because it was a strong field Baxter started 60th but managed to jump to 29th in the first run. In the second run, he started second and took advantage of the pristine, untouched course to climb to 11th. He was happy but knew he could have done better. Towards the end of the run, Baxter's skis were disintegrating under him. After the race Baxter met with the Rossignol technicians.

"You've got to start making the 170s again," he told them.

"No Alain, you've got to start using the 177s. Everyone else likes them," he was told.

"But I don't like them! Please make some me some more 170s."

It was frustrating for Baxter. He was training well but was being let-down by his equipment. He did win a Nor-Am Cup in mid-November, but the next day crashed out of a second race. He went to the second World Cup meet of the year with mixed feelings.

"I didn't know what to expect in Vail. I started 75th in the Slalom, which would be my main focus from now on. I skied okay on the top part of the course which had been cut up, but on the bottom part of the course I really started rocking. I got the 25th fastest split on the bottom half to end 40th. I didn't qualify for the second run but getting that top 30 split was massive for me at the time – it showed me I could cut it with the best in the world. But my skis had broken again. They just exploded on the ice or when I caught gates. They weren't built for that sort of punishment. God knows how much time they were costing me. Vail was a case of what could have been."

Baxter came away with the feeling that he was getting closer to qualifying for that elusive World Cup second run, however. All that was holding him back were his skis. After catching flu, Baxter took a fortnight off and returned to Aviemore to mull over his predicament. His world ranking was comfortably back inside the top 100 but like his skis, his confidence was shattered. He was back by mid-December at a World Cup in Italy. Again he missed qualifying for the second run. He repeated that performance in Slovenia a few weeks later but received welcome relief from his performances in the Europa Cup. Baxter finished 25th, 42nd, 16th and 19th in consecutive Europa Cup Slaloms, before recording a 12th (GS) and 2nd (Slalom) at the Austrian Nationals. The results brought priceless ranking points.

In Baxter's next seven FIS and Europa Cup races he would finish only once, a 3rd place in Italy. He was growing increasingly disillusioned. He was skiing well but was being let down by his equipment. He'd tried to reason with Rossignol but until one of the top sponsored skiers decided they preferred the 170, Baxter would have to like it or lump it. He was not paid to wear the brand, but he did receive free equipment and thought Rossignol deserved a little loyalty. Baxter battled on in vain but his patience was quickly running out.

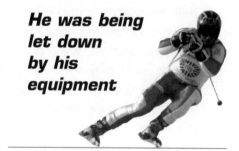

He was being let down by his equipment

In late February he recorded 1st, 3rd, 6th and 15th place finishes in FIS Races. Yet even in the races he won he felt uncomfortable on the skis. It couldn't go on.

Salvation came after winning the Slalom at the British Championships. Baxter chanced upon a couple of sets of Salomon Factory skis that retiring skier, Pete Walters, had left behind. They were even shorter than the fragile 170cm skis Baxter had been using all season and despite not being the most up to date Factory skis, Salomon were known to have the best short ski that year. Baxter knew an opportunity when he saw it and he set about preparing the skis for his next race. With little practice, Baxter came 3rd in his first race on the skis. He felt like a new skier, the responsive equipment giving him the type of feel and control he hadn't enjoyed all season.

Any vestige of loyalty to Rossignol that Baxter had went out of the window then. Baxter had given them ample opportunity to produce a ski he liked. Baxter left for a tour of Canada with unmatched enthusiasm. He arrived jetlagged and tired and woke the next morning for the first run of a Nor-Am Cup on his borrowed skis. He came down in 4th. In the second run Baxter blew everyone away, winning the race and $1,600. Afterwards he called a surprised Walters to thank him for the 'loan' of skis.

In the second Slalom of the weekend Baxter skied into a comfortable 0.4 second lead but would later be disqualified for straddling. It mattered little. His confidence was slowly returning and the new ranking list showed Baxter at 63 – his highest ever ranking. He went on to finish the season strongly with four more FIS top tens. It was all systems go.

Because he'd been uncomfortable on his skis for most of the season it hadn't felt like a massively successful year but Baxter's ranking spoke for itself. Schwaiger was ecstatic but Baxter would later reflect that the season had been a missed opportunity.

"I didn't feel that I was performing to my best but I was still getting results in the Europa Cup that I'd never had before. I was ranked in the top 30 at that level but could have done so much better if I'd had solid skis. That really could have been my breakthrough year in the World Cup because I was so close to qualifying on a couple of occasions. My ranking could have been lower too if I hadn't missed races with flu."

But Baxter was happy to have lowered his ranking by so much and treated himself to an end of season trip to visit his mother and stepfather in Courchevel. It was a chance to unwind and escape the pressures of the ski scene.

"Stork was working in Courchevel so I went to see him and mum and Kenny. Mum had a barbeque on the piste one day so Stork and I borrowed some snowboards and went up. We had a few drinks and said, 'Last one down buys the beers.' I grabbed onto Stork to try and speed up but my board ended up between his legs and we went over. I was wearing my mum's jacket and a pair of shorts and was in a pile at the bottom of the piste.

Stork looked over and said, 'Not bad for the 63rd best skier in the world!'"

After his short break Baxter returned to Austria to test skis. He was determined not to have another season dogged by equipment problems. He was 26 and couldn't afford to waste any more opportunities. He had a preference for Salomon skis after his recent success but he'd also seen team-mate Moulder-Brown have a good season on Head. Fischer made all the running, however.

"Fischer were keen to get me on their skis as they'd seen how much I'd improved. I liked the idea because I knew the guys at Fischer well. Their skis were not quite up to Head's though. I told Fischer that they needed to make them slightly thinner in the middle – then they'd have a shorter radius and turn quicker. I wanted to give them a chance so we arranged to race them against the other skis I liked. The Heads felt far better immediately and there was no doubt in my mind that that was what I wanted to be skiing on but there was a slight complication – Fischer were offering to pay me. It was only a few thousand pounds but it would have been my first ski contract. It was a massive offer at the time but I knew that Head were the better skis. Head hadn't offered me a contract though. It was a tough decision but there was no way that I was going to take skis just for the money. What was the point when I'd been trying so hard all my life to get somewhere in skiing? I couldn't sell out at the first opportunity."

Baxter stuck to his principles. The best ski won the day and it felt good to lay his equipment problems to rest. It had also felt good to have had the offer of a paid contract. It proved that people were taking note of his progress. He was starting to be noticed by the press too, but Baxter's main cause for excitement that summer was his ranking. It meant that his start number for the World Cup races the following season would be that much better. For the first time in his career he could dream about mounting a serious challenge on skiing's elite.

> CHAPTER 7

FACING A BAN

HANDING BACK THE MEDAL
THE SUPPORT OF OTHER SKIERS
AN APPEAL FUND IS LAUNCHED
THE BAN IS ANNOUNCED

7   **FACING A BAN**

After the emotional press conference at the site of his unforgettable homecoming parade, Baxter was reunited with his friends and family at a dinner in his honour. It was more like a funeral wake. There was nothing to say on the matter and the hurt was so raw for Baxter that it was too early to dissect the IOC verdict. It was universally accepted that they had got it wrong. The newspapers were unanimously behind the Scot, their pages full of words of support. Johan Eliasch, chairman of Head, told *The Scotsman*, "It is very disappointing news. It is an ill-judged decision. He is a terrific guy and we have absolutely no plans to change our sponsorship position. He has the support of the entire ski community."

Pete Wishart, SNP's Westminster spokesman on culture, media and sport said, "It is clear he is the victim of an innocent mistake, and the IOC have reacted far too harshly."

Speaking in *Scotland on Sunday*, Fergus Ewing, Baxter's local MSP, said, "I am urging Jack McConnell (Scotland's First Minister) to make direct representations to the IOC in order to correct this grave injustice which has been committed against a modern Scottish hero and role model for our young people."

HANDING BACK THE MEDAL

It was immensely comforting for Baxter to see the widespread support. He was devastated to have lost his medal, and have the record-breaking result wiped from the record books forever. The main concern of those who knew him best was how he would handle it. There was no predicting what his knee-jerk reaction would be. He'd handled the period up to Lausanne in a remarkably mature and philosophical manner but there was still a chance that the latest blow could push him over the edge. One can only imagine what it felt like to have something which you've coveted all your life ripped unceremoniously from your grasp. The IOC could dress it up any way they wanted. By taking Baxter's medal they were branding him for life as a cheat.

"I gave the medal to the BOA as soon as we'd heard the verdict. There was no point hanging onto it any longer. I'd had it for just over three weeks but I'd only looked at it when people wanted to see it. It was in its box most of the time so I wasn't that attached to it at all. From when I went to Norway the medal was tarnished. It didn't mean the same to me. I won't lie – of course it would have been great to keep it, to have something to treasure – but it wouldn't have been the same if I had. I didn't cherish it. What was important to me were the memories of Salt Lake. How I got there, being there, doing it, and all the things which followed, everything up until my homecoming. Anything after that I decided to put to the back of my mind and forget about."

I won't lie... it would have been great to keep it

Baxter's views on the medal may seem extreme and unsentimental. Of course, on one level Baxter is like anybody else: he was driven to distraction. But blocking out what had happened was a survival mechanism and was the only way he was ever going to get through it. How could he ever come to terms with the inadvertent nature of his offence? He hadn't known he was taking a banned substance, hadn't got any benefit from it, and would never feel as if he had cheated. What more was there to say? It was the IOC who should have had the sleepless nights for crushing the dream of a young athlete – a dream which epitomised the very spirit of the Olympics.

But Baxter also had a certain mindset shared only with fellow elite athletes. It is a disposition which separates those at the top of their sport from the also-rans. To reach the upper echelons you have to be extraordinarily resilient. You have to stare in the face of defeat and disappointment again and again, then get up, dust yourself off, and tell yourself that you'll succeed one day. Yes, it makes success more sweet when it does finally come but it also means that success becomes less about the medal, the reward, and more about the road travelled. Baxter would never have kept going through his fifteen years of struggle if it was just about having a medal round his neck. So few people ever win an Olympic medal that it would be folly to fixate on it. Baxter's bronze was not just about the 1 minute 42.32 seconds of that race. It was about all the fence-posts he'd hammered in to earn money for summer camps, it was about all the meals he'd missed and nights he'd slept in the back of his car in order to attend races, it was about the years of self-improvement and the milestones he'd passed. The IOC could take away his medal but they could never take away the sense of achievement. He'd take that with him to the grave.

That Baxter didn't implode is a credit to him. Lesser men might have crumbled. Ski veteran and lifelong friend John Clark, who would later try and persuade him to take his case to the Court of Arbitration for Sport, has his own view on how the news affected Baxter.

"Of all the people this should not have happened to, it shouldn't have happened to Alain because he would never cheat at anything. In the same breath, it was only Alain, and his particular mindset that could have handled it."

Those who knew Baxter best found his pragmatic approach bordered on the brutal. But they respected that it was how he had to be to survive the ordeal. The determination which had enabled him to train 365 days a year, 6 hours a day, the sheer single-mindedness with which he'd clawed his way up the rankings, somehow enabled him to see the medal loss as just another small set-back in an unerring path to the top of the sport. Lesley McKenna, an athlete renowned for her own mental toughness in driving the development of women's snowboarding, was one of the few people who could truly relate to what he was going through. She'd seen first hand how hard he had worked to get on that podium. But even she was baffled by her cousin's resilience.

"I couldn't have gone through what Alain did. It would have destroyed me. I think he set an amazing example by holding his head up high and not being changed by it. He didn't say more than a couple of sentences to me after he lost the medal. That's the way he is. You're not going to have a long conversation with him about things like that. But I knew what he was going through. I said to him, 'Oh well, it's only a bit of metal.' It may seem flippant but he knew I wasn't belittling what he had achieved. What I was saying was that what he achieved was way more than what that medal could ever represent. If people think that Salt Lake was the highlight of Alain's career then they would be selling him very short."

Clark's and McKenna's insights are astonishingly accurate. The medal was merely a token of victory to Baxter. It wasn't victory itself. Taking it away was not taking away what he'd achieved in Salt Lake or throughout his career. Baxter will argue that Salt Lake is not even his best result, citing instead his 4th place at the World Cup Finals the season before. It was the reward for consistently skiing well at the highest level over an entire season. There was no bigger race in the sport. Yet, Baxter doesn't seek to diminish what an Olympic medal represents. He is the first person to visit schools to encourage children to take up skiing, to dare to dream of the Olympics. And indeed his visit to Aviemore Primary School the day before he received the crushing news from the BOA is more telling about Baxter's character than first meets the eye. Baxter never forgot his medal because he is absent-minded. He'd forgotten it because the Olympic dream was alive inside him, not trapped inside a piece of semi-precious metal. He'd gone to the school to speak about the Olympic experience but all the pupils wanted was to see the medal. The incident hadn't surprised Baxter's mother:

"It was typical of Alain. He is not materialistic in any way. He never has been. All his trophies from his career are in our house except those he has given to sponsors or other family members. That typifies Alain's modesty. He has never been the type to display them. He knows in his mind what he is achieving without needing the silverware to prove it. If I didn't display his trophies they'd be in a box in his garage. His Olympic medal was no different. You only have to look at where the medal was on the night of the ceremony. Noel had it round his neck all night and slept with it in his pocket. At the homecoming, Ian wore it and still had it the next morning. That Alain didn't get attached to it helped when it came to giving the medal back. I actually kept the bag it came in. Alain's not interested but I thought at least we have something to remind us."

He knows what he is achieving without needing silverware to prove it

Baxter's seeming ambivalence to the medal is not as strange as it seems. Football World Cup winners have been known to auction their medals for charity or personal gain. Muhammad Ali is rumoured to have thrown his Olympic gold medal into the Ohio River after being refused service at a Louisville diner. We hear time and time again of actors using Oscars as door-stops, their accomplishment embodied in the film not the diminutive statue. Speaking one year on from the Athens Olympics to *Observer Sport Monthly*, multiple gold medal-winning swimmer, Michael Phelps said: "I only saw my medals for the first time since the Olympics the other day."

THE SUPPORT OF OTHER SKIERS

Another saving grace for Baxter was the universal support of his peers. Ever since the story had broken there had been a chorus of support from the ski circuit. Not a single negative comment was heard from a fellow skier throughout the ordeal. Skiing legends like Herman Maier, Bode Miller, and indeed Benjamin Raich, who was to receive Baxter's bronze, came out in support of the Scot. His rivals on the slopes were 100 per cent behind him and that meant everything to Baxter. Alpine skiing is a sport like no other. The prestige and respect of your fellow skiers counts above all else. Skiers travel the world together, train and race together. It is a sport where your fiercest rival is your best friend. Racers ski against the elements, against the uncertainly of hooking a gate, of serious injury, of equipment failure, no matter how well they're skiing. For Baxter, to have a quorum of support from those skiers was the only endorsement he needed. And Baxter was itching to get back to the slopes. It was a case of moving on, of looking forward, despite the growing pressure on him to appeal the IOC's ruling. But Baxter would make no snap decision. He threw himself into training before departing for a summer camp in Italy.

"After not skiing for over a month I was fast straight away. It was ironic – I was staring a long ban in the face but was skiing better than ever. Australian skier, Jono Brauer, who trains with us said, 'You b**tard! You don't ski for a month and you're a second quicker than me straight away.' It was good to be back on skis."

Being back on the slopes opened Baxter's eyes to the horror that a long ban from the International Ski Federation (FIS) could bring. The prospect disturbed him more than losing ten Olympic medals. Anything over 12 months and his career would effectively be over. Baxter would have to wait a few agonising months, until June 3, to hear his fate. He returned from Italy to find there was a growing lobby urging him to fight the IOC. He was loathe to even give any more interviews on the subject, let alone launch a costly and time-consuming appeal. Far from being a political campaigner, he preferred to shun the limelight. He was a skier first and foremost. He knew nothing else.

The worst part of Baxter's ordeal was that people wanted him to become a poster boy for anti-IOC demonstrations. It wasn't his style. MSP Fergus Ewing had planned to raise the issue at First Minister's Question Time in the Scottish Parliament but was forced to renege at the insistence of Baxter. When cousin Lesley and Margot McDonald MSP organised a protest at Edinburgh Airport where IOC President, Jacques Rogge, was arriving for a rugby international, Baxter was nowhere to be seen.

Baxter could ignore all the public attacks on the IOC but he couldn't ignore the fact that the deadline to decide on whether to appeal to the Court of Arbitration for Sport (CAS) was looming. As much as he wanted to clear his name, what he feared most was not losing the appeal, rather the crippling legal bill. It had already cost over £10,000 for the Lausanne hearing. The next stage of appeal would require months of preparation, could cost nearer £100,000 and the support of the BOA and the BSSF could not be guaranteed.

"Launching an appeal was my choice to make but whether I succeeded or not had no bearing on the fact that I couldn't afford it. I'd only just earned a little bit of money from skiing. I didn't know if I could put everything into paying for lawyers. But everyone was saying, 'You've got to fight it to the end'. I was nodding but thinking, 'Who's going to pay for this?' I was really scared. I wasn't even sure if I wanted to go through it all again. What if CAS agreed with the IOC? The people who mattered to me – family, friends, fellow skiers – already knew I was innocent. What did I stand to gain?"

Baxter was right. To appeal was a gamble with no guarantee of justice. The only guarantee was that it would be expensive. To go to sport's highest court he would need the best legal representation that money could buy. He had just received a significant bonus for the bronze medal from Drambuie and

Head had agreed to pay half of its bonus in light of Lausanne. But Baxter had lost Lottery funding to the tune of £70,000 per season. Left to his own devices, this would have been the first fight of his career that Baxter would have walked away from. It would be Clark, who was Athlete's Representative at the Federation, who would put most pressure on Baxter to appeal. Only he can explain why he was moved to do so.

"I've known Alain since the day he was born. His parents are friends with my brother, Hugh. I never actually coached Alain but I followed his career closely. We're good friends. When I heard he'd failed the test it felt like a close relative had died. My heart just sank. I knew he was innocent, but that Lausanne was going to be a total disaster. There are many reasons why I got involved. Alain was not my life's work.

Launching an appeal was my choice to make

But to have been part of the system that helped one person get in the position to win this country's first Olympic skiing medal meant a lot to me and to other people. There were those that got injured, that couldn't afford to keep racing, that just didn't have the talent. We've even had people killed racing. Alain's win was for all those people. What he achieved meant everything. It was the pay off for all the investment in time, money, emotion. And because we were friends it was personal too. I couldn't have the IOC tell me that what I'd worked for all my life was a sham."

Sensing his growing interest, McNeilly put Clark in touch with Arnold Beckett. Beckett had briefly advised on Baxter's defence before Lausanne, having been referred to McNeilly by Drambuie, but was thought too controversial to use as expert witness. Beckett persuaded Clark that an appeal to CAS would have a great chance. Clark relayed the conversations to Baxter who remained unconvinced:

"You know me John, I just want to get back on the snow and train. I don't want to spend all summer in a lawyer's office."

AN APPEAL FUND IS STARTED

Clark explained to Baxter that the appeal would cause minimal disruption to his training schedule. The IOC had accepted his story at Lausanne. He would just need to answer occasional questions in the run up to the hearing and make a short statement on the day. Having come to the end of a contract with the British Snowboard team, Clark was prepared to put in some work on the appeal for free. Baxter trusted Clark. He had no ulterior motive for helping, just the skier's best interests.

"John's enthusiasm really rubbed off on me and got me thinking. In a court of law you are innocent until proven guilty. I was guilty in the eyes of the IOC as soon as the results came through. Even a murderer is innocent until he's tried. More and more I was thinking that CAS was the way to go, but there was no way I could afford it."

Clark respected Baxter's fears. He'd seen him struggle for years and it wasn't right to expect him to sacrifice his meagre life savings. But Clark knew that there was a mass of goodwill for Baxter. People had been calling the Federation and pledging donations to support any possible appeal. *The Daily Record*, too, received numerous unsolicited donations from readers. One reader called pledging £2,000. It was too good to be true and Federation finance director, Alan Hartley, set up the Alain Baxter Appeal Fund. It was a pivotal moment. Clark informed Baxter of the development. His mind was made up.

"Once the fund started that was it. Even though the appeal would eventually cost me thousands of pounds of my own money it wouldn't have happened at all without the fund. I can't thank people enough for that."

With Baxter committed, Clark set about trying to secure the support of the Federation and the BOA. Clark was buoyed by the growing coffers in the fund but he would have been foolish to presume that it would cover all Baxter's costs. The BOA and BSSF needed to be fully behind him too. Yet Clark knew that an appeal to CAS, and the inherent costs, would begin to impact on both organisations' agendas. Lausanne had already been costly to the BOA and it was anyone's guess whether its continued support could be relied upon. It was required to participate in Lausanne as Baxter was a Team GB athlete. The appeal to CAS was made as an individual. The BSSF, too, would be no pushover. Its priority was to fund skiing, not lengthy legal battles. Clark would have one shot at convincing each of the importance of their support.

The perfect stage for Clark's plea to the BSSF came a matter of days later. It would be his last meeting with the Federation board as Athlete's Representative and he didn't intend to waste the opportunity.

"I asked the board for its full backing. There was a stand-off and it was clear that we could not count on its unanimous support. I knew that although Fiona was behind Alain there was a potential conflict of interest that would limit what she could do and say. I knew that the board members had their own agendas that would take precedence over the athlete. The appeal process would strike at the very heart of the Olympic family which could have repercussions for the Federation."

Despite the lukewarm response, the BSSF did pledge £5,000 toward Baxter's appeal. It was a gesture that it could little afford and which ate into what little available budget it had. So, over and above any reluctance at board level, its hands were tied. In particular, it didn't please McNeilly.

"We might have helped more but there was some disagreement because Alain had failed a drugs test, all be it unwittingly. You could say that he had brought the Federation and the sport into disrepute. But I had a far more emotional view of how we should support him. I don't think we could have underwritten further legal fees. Any money we put behind the appeal would have eaten into someone else's funding."

Clark had mixed feelings about what to expect from the BOA. On one hand he knew that it was intrinsically linked to the IOC. They were inter-dependent. Craig Reedie was not only Chairman of the BOA but one of the IOC's most esteemed members. He may have already known that London would launch a bid for the 2012 Games, for which he'd need to curry favour with as many members as possible, something the appeal could jeopardise. On the other hand, Clark had known Simon Clegg since 1984. He'd always found him to be fair and had called on his help before Salt Lake when it was revealed that the US Snowboard Team was planning to train covertly on the half-pipe to be used in the Games. Clegg had pulled out all the stops so Clark's team could fly to Utah to train there too. However, when the clandestine plan was revealed and both teams were caught out by the IOC, Clegg had stood by Clark.

John Clark being interviewed by Channel 4

Clark met with Clegg at the Wandsworth HQ of the BOA in late March. The Executive Board was due to meet later that day and Clark asked Clegg where the organisation stood on the matter. Clegg told Clark that it was his intention to request that the board cover 25% of all the legal costs. Clark was taken aback. It was more than he'd hoped possible but he had a niggling feeling that the proposal would be met with opposition.

"I thanked Simon but said that if the board refused I wanted to look the chairman in the eye and ask him why. After our meeting Simon went to meet the board. Some minutes later the door swung open and Reedie walked in. I knew that it was time to stand up and be counted. I told him that it would be key to Alain's appeal to put pressure on the IOC to finally perform the Isomer Separation Analysis. I could see he was a man under pressure but I pressed him, 'I need you to use your influence with your fellow members of the IOC to persuade them that they must perform the test.' Reedie was indignant. He said, 'You've no idea what you're getting into,' and he stormed out of the room. He returned shortly after and the conversation continued. I don't

remember the exact words but he started lecturing me: 'Do you think that you're going to be able to do this by rattling collection tins up and down the streets of Aviemore?' I told him to go and vote as he saw fit. We'd appeal by ourselves if that's what it took."

Despite the heated exchanges, the Executive Board voted to support the appeal. It is alleged that Reedie's vote swung things in Baxter's favour. Though Clark felt that Reedie's attitude had been aloof, in retrospect, perhaps he was merely highlighting that if the appeal was to be done it would need to be done properly. Like Baxter's parents all those years before, perhaps Reedie was trying to avert future disappointment by highlighting the enormity of the enterprise from the outset. No-one knew the machinations of the IOC better.

The support of the BOA was to be critical

The support of the BOA was to be critical. Clegg's pledge translated to the contribution of Sara Friend's time and expertise. It was the first time the BOA had supported an athlete at CAS and bringing it into the fold also opened the door for Adam Lewis and Michael Beloff QC to join the appeal team. They were both heavy hitters in sports law and human rights. The two were already up to speed on Baxter's case so it only remained to decide whether to expand the embryonic arguments used in Lausanne or change tack altogether. At the outset Clark did not discuss what the eminent lawyers would be paid. Their standard fees were far beyond what Baxter and the appeal fund could ever meet but Clark proceeded with blind faith in the massive goodwill toward Baxter.

Clark was being steered in the appeal by renowned Scottish defence QC, Bill Taylor, who had worked on the Lockerbie bombing trial. Taylor, who had been introduced to Clark by Frank Strang, a friend and trustee of the Alain Baxter Appeal Fund, had already gone on record saying that if the CAS appeal failed he would represent Baxter *pro bono* in the European Court of Civil Rights. Taylor's counsel gave Clark the confidence to hold his own with the sharpened legal minds of Friend, Lewis and Beloff back in London. Clark was also guided by Beckett. Friend was less enamoured by him than Clark.

Throughout April, after Baxter's appeal was officially lodged, Clark, Friend, Lewis and Beloff worked on the draft submission which would lay out the grounds for the appeal. Beloff and Lewis were keen to pursue the notion that, as Baxter only had a small trace of a banned substance in his system, the punishment should have been minor too – but it was dismissed by Clark and Baxter. He felt that it was an admission of guilt. Proportionality would form part of the appeal but would not be a key argument. Instead Clark, Friend and Lewis agreed that they should elaborate on what they'd argued in Lausanne in the hope that CAS would provide a more sympathetic ear. They'd argue that:-

1) The IOC had not established that what was found in Baxter's sample was actually a prohibited substance.
2) On proper construction of the IOC rules, it needed to establish fault in Baxter – and had failed to do so.
3) In any event, given the facts of this case, the sanction of disqualification was disproportionate.

They were simple arguments with solid science to back them up and Friend worked tirelessly to put together the legal and scientific construction of the case. It required many hours of trawling through reference books and Pharmacopia. The BOA became alarmed at the time-consuming nature of the appeal – Friend's other work began to pile up on her desk – but felt that once it had pledged its support it was only right to give it in full. Arnold Beckett's growing involvement, however, remained a sticking point for Friend.

"I knew that if we submitted a statement from Beckett he could have been called to give evidence. That was the last thing we wanted. Though he'd told us he'd left the IOC Medical Commission voluntarily, I had reason to believe that this wasn't entirely true. I knew that the IOC would have a file on him and could have completely discredited him as an expert witness and our case along with it. I believed it wasn't a risk worth taking."

Friend wanted to continue using Finkle as expert witness. He shared many of Beckett's views and was highly regarded by the IOC. As the weeks passed the issue drove a wedge between the team. It frustrated Clark.

"Beckett was prone to going off on tangents which frustrated Sara. Adam

Alain Baxter being interviewed by Channel 4

took me into a separate room one day and explained that she was pulling her hair out because of the tension – there was some history between Beckett and the IOC which she was party to. It was implied that if we insisted on using Beckett as our expert witness, the BOA would pull its support. I decided to call the BOA's bluff and they stayed on-board but it later became apparent that Finkle was the man for the job."

The team worked throughout April on Baxter's appeal. It was a full-time job for Clark and Friend. An initial submission had to be delivered to CAS by May 3, 2002, after which time the IOC and Baxter's team would trade written arguments. Only then, on September 5, would Baxter get his day in court. Clark was happy to provide Baxter with regular updates by telephone as the appeal gathered momentum.

"I never ceased to be amazed with how Alain went about his training. He was still waiting to hear from FIS about the ban and the appeal was hanging over his head but I'd call him up on a glacier somewhere and he wouldn't even ask me about the appeal. I would have to bring it up. I've scratched my head a lot about that. He just seemed to be able to switch-off completely."

But Clark's efforts were not going unnoticed. Baxter couldn't have been more grateful.

"John was brilliant and the work the lawyers put in on my behalf was above and beyond what anyone could have expected. It left me free to train which blocked everything else out and let me get on with my life."

Being back on the slopes had been a welcome tonic for Baxter. He bumped into numerous fellow racers and they all had a sympathetic word for him or a derogatory comment about the IOC. In his world he could walk with his head held high. It was only in the corridors of the IOC that he need feel shame. Donations were still trickling into the Appeal Fund and his Aunt Penny had raised £4,000 through an auction of Olympic memorabilia. His campaign received a further boost when Scotland supporters paid for a pitch-side advertising hoarding at the Scotland v Nigeria match at Pittodrie

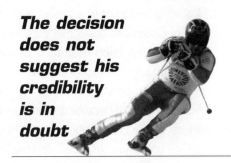

The decision does not suggest his credibility is in doubt

Stadium, Aberdeen bearing the message, 'The Tartan Army Supports Alain Baxter'. Baxter was humbled by their support. Even The Queen gave Baxter her tacit seal of approval. He was invited to a party at Holyrood Palace in Edinburgh on May 23. Baxter was supposed to wear his Team GB outfit but refused. He also refused to do any interviews arranged by the BOA. It was as political as Baxter would get. He won't be drawn on the significance of his actions but his mother has her own view:

"Alain wasn't anti-BOA but I think he reflected that they could have put more pressure on the IOC in the first place."

Baxter also thought it crass and inappropriate to highlight that The Queen thought him suitable company for afternoon tea, though the IOC branded him a drug cheat.

THE BAN IS ANNOUNCED

With the CAS appeal progressing steadily, all attention turned to FIS in early June. After Lausanne, the IOC had lobbed the ball into FIS's court, albeit with a glowing recommendation. It was incongruous, considering its harsh treatment of Baxter. Director General of the IOC, François Carrard, wrote a memo to FIS second-in-command, Sarah Lewis, on April 8, 2002 stating:

"Please note that the decision taken by the IOC Executive Board in the matter of Mr Alain Baxter does not suggest that his credibility is in doubt."

It gave grounds for hope but McNeilly was getting mixed messages from FIS. Knowing Sarah Lewis, a former boss at the Federation, McNeilly had the ear of the organisation. Lewis had even wept when Baxter had won his medal but Lewis gave no impression that FIS would go easy on Baxter. The FIS Council was scheduled to meet on June 3, 2002, and in the run up to the meeting McNeilly put pressure on Lewis to show leniency because it was both Baxter's first offence, and because it was a case of unintentional doping – circumstances which, by the FIS rulebook, merited a three month ban. Such a ban would have ended on August 18, 2002, leaving Baxter free to participate in the first two World Cup races of the season on November 24-25, 2002.

When FIS announced its decision soon after the council meeting, banning Baxter until December 15, 2002 – a seven month ban – McNeilly was incandescent with rage. Having stated in its official press release that it concurred with the IOC that Baxter's was a case of 'unintentional doping', FIS were obliged to administer a ban of no more than three months.

"It was immediately obvious that they'd applied the ban in such a way that it was longer than it should have been. Graham Bell said immediately that we had to fight it. I couldn't get hold of Alain so I called John and told him to tell Alain not to speak to the press until we decided what we were going to do. Eventually, I wrote to FIS Chief Executive, Gian Franco Kasper, to say we would go to CAS unless he reconsidered the ban. He wrote back saying that he believed the ban was appropriate."

Baxter was devastated when Clark gave him the news. From the dark days when a two year ban seemed likely, he'd come to terms with the more attractive prospect of missing merely the early season races in the Southern Hemisphere. He already felt punished after missing the end of the previous season. The seven month ban had far-ranging implications. Baxter's pre-Salt Lake ranking was 18. His Olympic result would have slashed that further had he not been disqualified. Resultantly, his ranking tumbled to 43. It was imperative that he get back competing as soon as possible to reclaim some ground. His priority was to be back for the first World Cup in November.

Despite this, Baxter didn't fancy another costly and time-consuming appeal to CAS. The IOC appeal was already pushing the team to the limit. McNeilly understood Baxter's worries but was further enraged when she finally saw the written outcome of the FIS ban on its website. A handful of other skiers had been banned for different offences and the duration of their bans was stated clearly alongside the dates for which their bans applied. Baxter's merely mentioned the dates between which he would be banned. Not the duration. Omitting the length of the ban was naïve and ambiguous. After digesting this information, Baxter realised that he had no choice but to fight FIS.

"I was shocked by the ban. It was longer than expected. If I couldn't compete until mid-December my status as a World Cup skier would be under threat. I'd worked so hard over the previous two seasons to establish myself at the top level that I couldn't just accept it. It meant more money, more favours and more stress, but we had to appeal."

It fell to Clark to do the lion's share of the work for the appeal against FIS. Clark had worked non-stop since late March, and it wasn't time to start shirking the responsibility he'd volunteered for.

"I took the crux of Fiona's argument and turned it into a 25 page document. I hired Harper Macleod Solicitors to help. They were great but invoiced for £9,000. There wasn't enough in the Appeal Fund to cover it so Frank Strang settled the bill personally. Alain was never told about that, we said that the fund paid."

The Court of Arbitration for Sport convened on August 16 to rule on the appeal. It had not required the two parties to attend, as was normal practice, insteading demanding written submissions from both. FIS had been asked to clarify its application of Baxter's ban and responded thus:

One month at the end of the 2001/2002 season (during which there were no FIS World Cup Races for which he was qualified), one month competition period in the Southern Hemisphere (during which there are no FIS World Cup Races) and one month at the beginning of the 2002/2003 season until December 15th 2002 during which period he will be ineligible for two FIS World Cup Slaloms.

Baxter's counsel was required to highlight why it believed this sanction had been wrongly applied. It drew the court's attention to the penalty for inadvertent doping in FIS's own Sanction Catalogue:

"Suspension from participation in all international ski competitions for three months for the first offence."

Baxter's counsel further underlined when the official start of the season was, as stated in the FIS Calendar, and proposed what relief they sought:

The first race on the FIS Calender for 2003 is to be held on July 25, 2002, at Valle Nevado (Chile).

Relief proposed by Appellant
A determination that the three month suspension imposed ends on 18th August 2002; two calendar months and seven days having been served between 23rd February and 30th April 2002 (the end of 2002 competition season) with a further period to be served from 25th July 2002 (the start of the 2003 competition season) until 18th August 2002, such that the three month suspension is served "during a fixed period during the actual or next competition season" in accordance with the FIS Medical Guide 2001/2002.

Reasons for relief
There is no distinction in the FIS Medical Guide 2001/2002 for doping offences between the different classes of international ski competition. It is submitted, therefore, that the sanction catalogue applies to all competitions in the FIS Calendar, and not only some classes, for example FIS World Cup races.

It is respectfully submitted that this Appeal should be dealt with as a matter of urgency, given that if the Appellant is unable to compete until 15th December 2002 his World Ranking may be affected.

It took little time for CAS to uphold Baxter's appeal and agree to the relief. He'd be eligible to compete in a matter of days. As soon as McNeilly was informed she called Baxter's coach. Schwaiger was jubilant:

"That's great news, hopefully we can get the same result with the medal appeal."

Baxter shared his coach's enthusiasm.

"I thought, 'That's it. That's all I want to hear. Forget about everything else and start thinking about your career again.' It was more important to get back racing, rather than get the medal back. I felt great. It felt like things were starting to go my way and that it was the first step on the road to justice. After waiting all summer, suddenly I was free to compete again. I was over the moon."

It was a major coup for Baxter and his team. CAS had showed a capacity for commonsense. It was the ray of light they needed after five months of solid spadework on the medal appeal. The countdown to Baxter's showdown with the IOC had begun. There was less than three weeks until they'd meet. It would be a battle of some of the world's leading legal and scientific minds to decide the fate of the greatest British skier to have ever lived.

> CHAPTER 8   **UNCHARTED WATERS**

SEASON 2000/2001
SEASON 2001/2002
OFF TO THE OLYMPICS

8   UNCHARTED WATERS

Despite being a top 100 skier, Baxter worked as a builder's labourer throughout summer 2000.

In early November, he flew out to Loveland, Colorado, for his most eagerly awaited season since his debut in 1990. It had taken ten years of toil, of financial struggle, of psychological torment and physical strain, but Baxter had hung in. He'd stood the test of time and was ready to reap the rewards. It would be Schwaiger's third season coaching Baxter, in which time he'd overseen the slashing of the Scot's world ranking. The Austrian coach had taken the Scotsman into uncharted waters.

SEASON: 2000/01

Age: 26/27
World Ranking: 61

Baxter's first race would be a Nor-Am Cup. Because of his impressive record on the tour he started the race in the top seven. Starting above numerous better-ranked skiers, it was a chance to score good ranking points. After training well in the summer on new skis, Baxter was confident of making the most of it.

"It was a perfect opportunity. I was skiing well but when I came to inspect the course it was ridiculous – really tight, with loads of sharp turns. I had two sets of skis to choose from – 170s and 175s. I said to Christian, 'I'm going to use the 170s.' He wasn't happy because I'd hardly skied on them.' 'No,' I told him, 'I feel comfortable on them.' I came out of the start gate and straddled the fifth gate. I thought, 'Christian is going to kill me.'"

Baxter would have just one more Nor-Am Cup from which to qualify for the first World Cup Race of the season in Park City. It was imperative not to crash or straddle again so Baxter decided to ski conservatively and was 17th.

It hadn't been the perfect preparation but at least he'd made the start list for the first World Cup.

At Park City, Baxter started 55 out of a field of 75. The odds were still stacked against him qualifying for his first ever World Cup second run but he felt good. Baxter came out of the start gate like a bullet from a gun but skied a poor top section and was only 50th fastest at the first split. But he started to fly on the bottom section and improved with every split to earn himself 17th position. He had skied the 2nd fastest time on the final split and had been the only skier from the low start positions to make up places. More importantly he'd just qualified for a World Cup second run for the first time in his career. It was a massive achievement for the Scot after all his years on the circuit and he was rightly in demand with the gathered press corps. The Scot didn't welcome the intrusion, however. He was already thinking about the second run.

It was a massive achievement for the Scot

"I was quite nervous as I waited to go up. Christian looked nervous too. He said. 'Don't take it easy and don't go crazy.' I thought, 'Cheers, that's great advice!' I went up to inspect the course, go through some of the gates, look at the pattern, the terrain changes. I was stunned – there were so few skiers there, only 30. For the first run there was 75. But for the second I could see the whole course. It was more sociable, you could have a little blether with some of the other racers. I thought, 'This is where I want to be.'

"By the time I got to the start line my nerves had gone. I had been more nervous for the first run because I had been skiing well during the summer and people were speaking about it. When I qualified the pressure was off. I was thinking, 'At last! That's been a long haul.' For the second run I didn't go full blast. I skied the top part a lot better than before but I was a bit hesitant on the lower section. I didn't want to crash. I really wanted to get my first World Cup finish. But I must have skied better than I'd though because I still got the 6th best time on the bottom section and was 21st. It was big news for British skiing and for Christian and me. It was the best result of my career."

After Park City, Baxter took advantage of a brief break in schedule to return to Aviemore. He'd been analysing his result and knew that he could do better. He was a born competitor and was never going to be happy being an also-ran, no matter what the level of competition. Baxter's friends thought differently. They were eager to celebrate their friend's long-awaited breakthrough. Baxter socialised so much during the visit that he boarded a plane to Finland still jet-lagged from the US. Flying to races was still a novelty for Baxter, who remembered the days he would have driven. A good field turned out at the Europa Cup in Levi, but Baxter recorded his best ever finish on the tour, coming 9th. The season was not yet one month old and Baxter had already broken new ground.

In Sestriere, ten days later, Baxter started 55th at the season's second World Cup. He was eagerly awaiting the new World Cup Start List to be published because his ranking had already improved to 41st. Because of Baxter's top 60 ranking, Britain was allocated an extra place on the World Cup start line, allowing team-mate Jonny Moulder-Brown to race in Sestriere. In the first run Baxter skied assuredly into 10th place. He was stunned. He'd qualified again, this time by some margin. Baxter was even happier to see Moulder-Brown ski down from the tail-end of the field into 20th to qualify for his first ever World Cup second run. It was an historic moment. The first time two British skiers had ever made the final of a World Cup. Baxter had been nervous on the first run due to the weight of expectation on his shoulders. Editors in the UK had dispatched their top correspondents to cover the race and he was in constant demand for interviews. He relaxed for the second run, perhaps too much, by his own admission, but was still 13th. It was an improvement on Park City and a career-best. Moulder-Brown was 17th.

Fiona McNeilly recalls the excitement that Baxter's ever-improving results caused: "I used to get so nervous when he raced. I'd sit in the office watching his races on Eurosport or the internet so I could get a release out as soon as he finished. I'd be jumping about if he was in a good position because I couldn't wait for the final run. I would have been happy to see it from any athlete but it was particularly nice to see it from Alain. We'd grown up together in the sport and I believed in his self-belief."

In training, Schwaiger pushed Baxter harder than ever. Now performing at the top level he started doing fewer and fewer lower ranking races and had one clear week to prepare for the next World Cup in Madonna on December 19. Conditions there were tough and it didn't auger well for Baxter who was still starting 55th.

"The course was rough and it took every ounce of my ability to come down in 28th. I wasn't happy at all. I was already putting pressure on myself to do better. But I was one of the first to go on the second run so I got my head together and hammered down. I skied far better and my time for that run was the second best of the day. I leapfrogged into 8th. It was my first ever top ten and Britain's first ever in World Cup Slalom. It was such a memorable day. After really going for it on the second run and achieving what I wanted, I felt like anything was possible at this level. This was where all the hard work started to pay off."

Baxter made it onto the back pages of the following day's newspapers. His success coincided with Madonna's wedding in a Scottish castle. It was a field-day for headline writers. 'Madonna does it in the Highlands and The Highlander does it in Madonna,' read one front page. Needless to say, at Christmas, Baxter received an even bigger welcome home than he had in November. His phone rang constantly. If it wasn't former team-mates calling to congratulate him, it would be potential sponsors. An auction of ski memorabilia had been arranged to help fund Baxter's World Cup campaign, but when Head offered him a paid contract with a bonus victory

Drambuie signed Baxter to the biggest sponsorship deal of his career

schedule, and Drambuie signed Baxter to the biggest sponsorship deal of his career, he requested that the £20,000 raised in the auction be spent on the rest of the team.

After Christmas, the British team settled into a new year-round base in Lofer, Austria. It was the first time that Baxter would have a permanent Alpine base. He would no longer have to lug all his belongings with him to every race. Another watershed for the Scot was about to occur. Having lowered his ranking to a groundbreaking 15th, Baxter became eligible for UK Sport World Class Performance funding. This made money available for a conditioning

coach, physio and serviceman for the first time. Everything was falling into place and, characteristically, Baxter shared his good fortune, making his support team available to the whole squad.

In January Baxter picked up where he had left off. At the World Cup in Wengen he started just outside the top 30 and finished an impressive 7th. Baxter's form was improving with every race. He even started dreaming of qualifying for the season finale, The World Cup Final, where the top 25 World Cup skiers, the Junior champion and four invitees battle it out for the prestigious Crystal Globe. No Brit had ever gone before. Baxter would be entering virgin territory to even qualify.

At Kitzbuehel for the next World Cup the crowd was 45,000-strong. Baxter had his own entourage of supporters there – Peter Steinlhe, who owned The Cairngorm Hotel, several friends and a bagpiper. Highlander-fever was gripping the Alps and Baxter battled hard to give his travelling support a top ten finish but could go no better than 13th. Two days later in Schladming, Baxter raced in the next World Cup in front of 60,000 people. It didn't get any bigger than this. World Cup skiers are huge celebrities across much of the globe, but nowhere more so than the Alps. Schladming would be the first

World Cup where Baxter would start inside the top 30, in 28th. Expectation was high and he stormed down, in the marauding style he was becoming renowned for, into 14th place. He had a good point from which to mount a challenge for a top ten finish and didn't disappoint, finishing 9th. With every race he felt more at home on the circuit.

The World Championships were held in St Anton in 2001. It was Baxter's fourth World Championships and much was expected. Bookmakers in Austria made the Scot their top outside bet for the Slalom. His mother and stepfather were full of hope too, travelling to see their son race amongst skiing's elite for the first time. Whilst there, they'd get a glimpse of his growing celebrity.

"There were thousands of people in St Anton. It was breathtaking. The locals were shouting as much for Alain as for the Austrians. It was a car free zone but one day we needed to get to the other side of the resort. A policeman stopped us at the barrier and told us to turn around so I said, 'But I'm the mother of The Highlander.' The policeman eyed me for a moment and then said, 'Oh, that's okay. Go straight through.'"

Baxter was as excited as his family. He relished being in contention at the big races. It was everything he'd always wished for since watching his grandfather's grainy Super 8 footage of the big Alpine races. Baxter had been racing on the same skis all season. It was a marked contrast to the year before when he went through a pair every run. More than a touch superstitious, he was loathe to change skis. They were right on the limit, however, with barely a millimetre of edge left. But Baxter had been skiing out of his skin on them and none of his new skis felt as good. It would be a decision he would regret. He came 16th – his best World Championship result – but could have done so much better.

Baxter should have learnt his lesson but at the next World Cup in Shigakoken, Japan, he used the skis again. He started 16th and a top ten finish was expected of him, yet he was only 18th after the first run. It had been the first time all season that Baxter had lost ground from his start position. He ended the race 18th and finally switched to new skis for a second Slalom the following day. But he went one worse, finishing 19th. He was both jubilant – the result had ensured qualification for the World Cup Finals – and disappointed – he had finished worse than his start number again. Suddenly Baxter was staring in the face of yet another crisis.

Baxter returned to Europe and, after beating many of the top racers in training, he relaxed and put things in perspective. How could he complain of a crisis when he'd be competing in his first World Cup Finals? His confidence was restored when he won the Austrian Championships in convincing style. He was as ready for the Finals as he'd ever be.

The World Cup Finals are considered, by skiers, as the blue riband event. It rewards consistent brilliance in the most unpredictable of sports. At the 2001 Finals in Are, Sweden, Baxter was required to take part in a picking ceremony to decide the start order of the top group. It was the first time he'd been ranked high enough to participate in the pre-race ritual but drew the short straw to start 14th out of the first 15 skiers. He was not encouraged. By the time he got down, the course would be like a ploughed field.

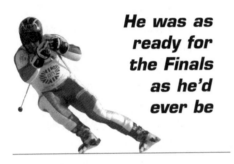

He was as ready for the Finals as he'd ever be

"I was really excited because I'd been beating the Austrians in training. Starting 14th would have been fine if it was icy but it was spring snow. I tried to put that out of my mind and felt confident coming out of the start gate. I skied well, everything was coming easy, and I came down into equal 3rd. I was over the moon. It was the first time I'd been in that position and I knew anything was possible in the next run. It was just a case of keeping my head."

That would be easier said than done:

"I was eligible for a £10,000 bonus from Drambuie if I finished third. I was trying to block it out of my mind, thinking, 'Get that right out of your head Baxter'. I made myself focus. It was my last big race of the season and all I needed to do was to ski like I'd been doing all year."

Baxter somehow managed to expel all his nerves before pushing off, and skied well to claim 3rd as his own with two skiers to come. He could hardly watch. The next skier down, Florian Seer of Austria, had broken through that year as well and as Baxter watched, expecting to be eclipsed by his time, Seer misjudged a gate, lost time and moved down to 12th. Baxter felt a mixture of relief and sympathy. It could have so easily happened to him. After Mario Matt, who was fastest in the first run, came down ahead of Baxter it meant he wouldn't make the podium. He contented himself with 4th place. There were many positives to take from the result. He had been just 4/10ths of a second from winning and it was the first time anyone from Britain had gone to the Finals, let alone finish in the top five. Baxter would also receive the accolade of the most consistent skier. He was the only one of the world's top 75 skiers to finish every World Cup race that season. It was an astonishing feat.

Cause for celebration too was Baxter's world ranking. He was 11th – the highest ever for a Brit. At the BSSF, McNeilly witnessed the impact of the news.

"Alain's success opened our eyes to the fact that we could get skiers to the top level. It helped our self-belief as an organisation. Alain had always had the potential, yet we thought top ten would be possible only in our wildest dreams. So when he was 11th we changed our expectations. Podiums suddenly became a real possibility."

There was much debate as to what had led to Baxter's great leap forward. The Federation's concentration on quality coaching was a major contributing factor as was Baxter's dogged dedication. Others thought that the purple patch could be attributed to something that Cairngorm Ski Club was getting right in the 1980s.

Throughout his career, Baxter's success on the slopes was underpinned by a strong network of support in his native Scotland. And it was there that he returned to toast the greatest season of his, or any other British skier's, career. Having visited every ski resort of any standing in the Northern Hemisphere in the previous ten years, it was to the familiar back-drop of Aonach Mor, in the shadow of Ben Nevis, where Baxter brought down the curtain on the 2000/01 season.

"There was a great atmosphere for two FIS Races and the British Championships. The latter was a disaster. At the third gate the binding flew off my ski. I got a re-run and the same thing happened again. After the race we all went back to the hotel. Ex-coaches and old sponsors like Hugh Robertson were there. I hadn't seen these guys for years and it was great, especially after the season I'd had. We drank a lot of whisky and reminisced. I'd just bought a motorbike and Hugh offered to sponsor the insurance. He said, 'What a great bike.' I said, 'Yeah, I've had it up to 150mph already!' His faced dropped: 'I don't want to know about that!'

"I was pretty hungover the next day, the first time I'd done that since I was 16. The point of me being there was to enable the younger British guys to win better ranking points and it had crossed my mind that it wouldn't be terrible if they beat me. But, despite feeling worse for wear, I didn't want to upset my sponsors. I was 2nd in the first race and won the second by the slenderest margin possible. It was good for everyone – the younger guys got good ranking points because a top 20 skier had only narrowly beaten them and no-one slagged me for skiing too slow."

Baxter wouldn't have missed catching up with his old benefactors for the world. He was grateful for every penny they'd given him. He had a personal connection with many of his sponsors that is rare in sport. For people like Robertson, the increased exposure for his company meant less than contributing to the fulfilment of a young boy's ambitions. That alone was worth every one of the tens of thousands of pounds spent. And it was all about following the dream for Baxter. He had never expected to make a living from the sport. But at the end of the season he received significant bonuses from Drambuie and Head and felt like the luckiest man in the world. As he relaxed at home, for a moment he could drift off and see himself as the wide-eyed 11-year-old in his first international race, then as the 17 year old slumming it in the back of his car. Back in the present and, looking at the sizeable cheques, he thought, 'Is someone really paying me to do this?' It had never been about the money. If it had, Baxter would have thrown in the towel long before. It was about testing himself again and again, plumbing the depths of the human spirit and bouncing back. Because of that, when success came it was that much sweeter. Baxter had earned the right to enjoy the view from the summit. But he wouldn't rest on his laurels. He'd tasted success and liked it.

SEASON: 2001/02

Age: 27/28
World Ranking: 11

The financial windfall brought about by the best season of his career afforded Baxter the luxury of not working during summer 2001. It was the first time he hadn't taken a seasonal job since he'd started skiing. Lottery funding was on stream too and Baxter had enough personal sponsors to allow him to train full-time, 'Like a professional athlete should'. Many of his rivals on the circuit would have been full-time since they were 15. It had taken Baxter twelve years to catch-up. Unless he had been blessed with great personal wealth or born in one of the big skiing nations he could never have done it any other way.

When not training in Aviemore, Baxter would spend most of the summer in Kaunteral, cycling on the Gros Glockner, Austria's tallest mountain. It was relentless but if the season before had been exciting, the one to come would be even better. It was Olympic year and Baxter couldn't wait to go to Salt Lake. Stage one of his lifelong dream had been attained – he'd represented his country at the Olympics. Dare he dream of stage two?

It was with great disappointment that Baxter learnt that Moulder-Brown was to quit the team. Though they'd followed different paths – Baxter had scrimped and saved for every hour on the snow, whereas Moulder-Brown had attended a specialist ski school in Austria from the age of 11 – they were united by a common dream. Skiing had been their lives. He'd be sadly missed by Baxter who would be back on his own again on the elite circuit. He would soon adjust. He'd had good friends retire before. Skiing was a fragile existence where your career could be taken from you in the blink of an eye.

Baxter attended two more camps in Saas-Fee and Pitztal late that summer and couldn't have been happier. It was a new experience to train full-time. It has often been said that many British skiers who have fallen by the wayside couldn't take the incessant training. It had never bothered Baxter whose endurance and commitment beggar belief.

Baxter was on Head skis again for the 2001/02 season. He got on well with the technicians there and was using a 164cm ski which had worked well on summer snow. Baxter's season would start in the familiar surroundings of Loveland Pass. He competed in two Nor-Am Cups, straddling in both. It was not how he'd hoped to start his Olympic season. The countdown to February 23rd was on. Baxter trained for five days before travelling to Aspen for the first World Cup Races of the season.

"I got drawn to start 11th for the first race. The conditions were strange – wet snow, big granules – my skis were bouncing around like crazy but I was feeling good and skiing fast in training. After the first run I'd slipped back a bit to 13th. After the second I went back to 15th. I was not happy. I mean relatively not happy – I was still 15th in a World Cup which would have been inconceivable one year earlier, but I knew I could have done better. That day Ivica Kostelic had won the race from starting 64th. No-one had ever won from that far back before and it showed how tight racing had become. I needed to keep on my toes because there were a lot of good skiers creeping up on me. The next day I was 1.8 secs out from the lead on the first run and didn't qualify. I was 33rd, thinking, 'Oh-oh. What's going on here?'"

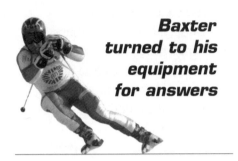

Baxter turned to his equipment for answers

Reassured by Schwaiger that he was skiing well, despite the result, Baxter turned to his equipment for answers. Baxter was on a Cap, or Moulded, ski. In the past, racers had traditionally used Sandwich skis, comprising layers of pressed wood, wrapped inside a plastic coating. Baxter had never liked the Cap skis and had suggested the season before that Head experiment with a Sandwich ski. They hadn't but now many of the other manufacturers were using the traditional method, Head took note and made a 155cm Sandwich ski which was excellent on soft snow, but which Baxter felt lacked the torsional stiffness required for hard snow. In layman's terms: they gave way under pressure. Head insisted that Baxter give them a go and he took the skis to Madonna in early December for the third World Cup of the season.

Baxter started in the top 15 again but was a little under two seconds off the lead. It was not enough to make the second run, something Baxter had now become accustomed to. The season before, Baxter had been 8th in Madonna, despite being two seconds slower than the winner. Now that margin wasn't enough to make the top 30. Baxter's ranking was on the slide too. He'd slipped to 17th. Baxter did a FIS Race and a couple of Europa Cup Slaloms ahead of the next World Cup in Kranjska Gora, Slovenia. He was 9th in the FIS Race but straddled in the two Europa Cups. He was getting frustrated. His skis didn't feel too bad. He blamed himself. Baxter's coach was baffled. Baxter appeared to be skiing well. He was technically perfect, he just didn't seem to have the speed of the previous season. Schwaiger employed the help of video analysis to get to the bottom of Baxter's dip in form. It didn't take many slow-motion re-runs to see that his skis were collapsing under him when he turned. His first instinct about the skis had been right.

Baxter took delivery of a third set of skis in the third week of December. It was unsettling that he couldn't get the right ski under him when he was skiing so well.

"I went to Slovenia with another pair of skis and I was getting pretty angry by then. The first course was set pretty straight. I was sick of it and decided to go for it, even if it meant landing on my head. I risked everything and was all over the place, but came down in 9th. I thought, 'You beauty! At last'. But the second run was really tight and twisty and I couldn't do a thing. I went from 9th to 27th. I was at boiling point. I went back to Head and said, 'Please make new skis for me. You have two weeks until the next World Cup in Adelboden.'"

His skis were collapsing under him when he turned

But Head didn't. In Adelboden, Baxter finished 25th, despite, again, feeling that he was skiing well. He was starting to finish behind skiers who had never beaten him before and his ranking slipped to 22. It had doubled in half a season. Baxter's frustration was palpable. Even the picking ceremonies which he had initially enjoyed were starting to grate.

"I was still in the top group, just, so had to do the picking ceremonies before every race. It's a real circus – sometimes you draw it out of a hat or have to abseil down and pick your number off a wall. I was not enjoying this at all because I was skiing badly. The new guys in the top group were really excited but I was getting p*ssed off, knowing that where I started wasn't going to make any difference to my result."

After Adelboden, Baxter threw down the gauntlet to Head – give him skis he could be competitive on or he'd look elsewhere. It wasn't an empty threat. Though Baxter had a reputation for loyalty amongst the manufacturers, everyone had their breaking point. World number 9, Killian Albrecht, had already paid his contract back to Head and moved to Nordica, so Head were starting to realise that they had better act quickly or lose Baxter just before the Olympics. Schwaiger, Baxter and his ski serviceman drove five hours from Adelboden to the Head factory, where they met chief ski developer and ex-racer Rainer Salzgeber.

"We sat for hours in the boardroom. I told Salzgeber I needed skis that were stiffer, torsionally stronger, with a modified sidecut and that I needed them for Wengen – the next World Cup race – otherwise I'd have to seriously consider my position. I was the only top skier left on Head so they finally saw the light. We left my serviceman there and told him not to come back without new skis."

Baxter's serviceman waited patiently and arrived back with just one pair. Baxter mounted the new skis on the Saturday morning and did ten practice runs, more than he would ever normally do the day before a race. By Saturday evening, Baxter was still not sure if he'd use the new ski in Wengen. Something didn't feel quite right. On the spur of the moment he asked his serviceman to mount a different plate (a component beneath the binding that improves dampening and ski control) on the new ski and he'd use them. It was a gamble but Baxter felt confident that the ski would feel right.

"I was starting 17th in Wengen and came down really far out from the leader in 12th. I met Bode Miller at the bottom and he said 'You were 1.5 seconds out on the top and only 1.49 out at the bottom. You must have been quickest on the bottom split.' I checked and I was 2nd quickest. At last I felt like something was working. After the second run I was 16th but had the 2nd fastest final split again. The top of the course had been set quite tight so I knew we needed to get the ski turning quicker, but at least I was smiling at the bottom of races again."

Between Wengen and the World Cup in Kitzbuehel one week later, Head worked overtime to deliver Baxter yet another set of skis. It would be his fifth of the season, compared with just two the season before. At Kitzbuehel, he raced on the improved skis but could only finish 18th. The skis still weren't turning to Baxter's liking and to compound matters, his back began to ache after every race. Years of repeated jarring had taken its toll. Baxter went to the final World Cup of the season in Schladming in late January. He'd tweaked the skis again and on the first run skied into a promising 14th place. He sniffed a top ten and as he flew down the second run his splits got better and better until he hooked a gate and fell. His back ached, but at least his form had returned. He would have almost certainly have been high in the top ten if he'd finished. It was the first run of the whole season where he'd felt as good on skis as the year before. He was back in the groove just in time for Salt Lake.

From Schladming, Baxter returned to Aviemore for a week of intensive physio. Olympic fever was growing in Britain, particularly in the Highland village, as Baxter, brother Noel and cousin McKenna were all going to Salt Lake. Journalists tried their best to coax a prediction out of Baxter. 'Are you going to bring back Gold?' they asked. 'I'm just going to do my best and see what happens,' Baxter would tell them. Inside he was thinking, 'Yeah, no problem. I'll bring home Britain's first ever ski medal!' Baxter knew it was a long-shot. There'd be over seventy skiers capable of putting in a medal-winning performance on the day and they'd be every bit as determined as the Scot. The BOA shared Baxter's caution, making him a Medal Zone candidate: a top six finish could be hoped for, at best, but Baxter was unlikely to come back with a medal.

With his back better and feeling confident, having regained a couple of ranking places in the newly published list, Baxter did something he'd promised himself for months. He'd made a personal pact to dye the Scottish Saltire flag into his hair if he was skiing well before the Games. Baxter thought it would be good to live up to his nickname: The Highlander. It was a bit of fun – not a protest about having to compete under the Union flag as was later implied. The day Baxter had his hair dyed in Aviemore he received an unexpected visitor.

"The first version of the Saltire didn't work but I had a tennis game planned so didn't wait to have it fixed. Halfway through the match all the blue dye started dripping down my face onto my shirt and the court. I was a mess. When I got back from tennis I was totally dehydrated after three hours in the hairdressers, and two hours on the court. As I pulled up at my house a man got out of a car and introduced himself. Who knows what he thought, because I was blue from head to toe. He was the drug tester from the Scottish Institute of Sport, there to conduct a random test ahead of Salt Lake. He had to stay by my side until I gave him a urine sample so I couldn't even shower but because I was so dehydrated I couldn't go. I could only manage a few drops so I drank litres of water but it took three sittings before he finally got what he came for."

Baxter's drugs test was clear, like every one he'd ever taken before. He didn't use any nutritional supplements or protein drinks at all and avoided anything that the powers that be disapproved of, even caffeine. The 2002 Winter Olympic Games had started by this time and Baxter watched the Downhill on television with a mix of excitement and detachment. The Slalom was not until the last day of the Games. As an exciting and unpredictable spectacle it is given pride of place. With two weeks until his race, Baxter left for Sappada, Italy. There, he matched his career-best Europa Cup result with a 7th place and finished 9th in his final pre-Olympic warm-up.

OFF TO THE OLYMPICS

Baxter arrived in Salt Lake some ten days before his event. The team wouldn't stay in the Olympic village, instead hiring a condo in nearby Park City, where the Slalom would be held. For some athletes the village is an integral part of the Olympic experience, but Baxter never saw the attraction. To him, the Games were about competition, about standing shoulder to shoulder with the best. It was the biggest stage a skier could ask for.

"I don't really go in for the Olympic village thing. I suppose it's good for the more social animals. Some people like mixing with athletes from different sports or countries but if you go to the Olympics to bring back medals I'm not sure it's the best place to be. I've been to six World Championships and two Olympics and I've never been to an opening or closing ceremony. It was the medal ceremonies which interested me. In any case, my race was 40 minutes from the village and it wasn't worth the hassle of getting caught in Olympic traffic every day when I could have been training or recovering. The coaches had done a recce two years before and found a house. We cooked for ourselves and ate together so it was a really good atmosphere."

In training, Baxter was skiing better than he had all season. He was peaking at just the right time and Schwaiger felt that his athlete was about to hit top form.

"The training was fantastic. I'd never seen Alain skiing so well. He was strong mentally, too. I knew if he skied like he was in training a medal was definitely possible."

Baxter still hadn't decided whether he'd ski in the GS at Salt Lake. Though it appears similar to Slalom it is as different as the 100m is to the 400m in athletics. The training and technique are different too. Baxter hadn't raced GS all season but had trained with team-mate Ross Green and felt good so decided to give it a go. It would still leave him a couple of clear days before the Slalom. It was a decision which would almost have grave consequences.

"I'll never forget that day. It was -15C but it was beautiful. Blue skies all day. The run we were training on was in the trees and in the afternoon Christian said, 'Be careful at the 10th gate. There's a little rise and the sun's getting lower so it's hard to see.' I'd never worried about seeing where I was going, as long as I knew the course, so I came down fast. I was skiing well but my outside ski went away from me right before the shaded area. I got the ski back under control but then I was at the knoll and the course just spat me out. I was upside down, backwards and doing the splits, three metres off the ground. I remember thinking, 'This is going to really hurt.' I tried to right myself but was still backward as I got nearer the trees. People die like this all the time. I finally landed just centimetres from the trees. I stood up but fell straight over because I was so dizzy. I checked my arms, my legs, my neck and realised that I was okay. Then I looked at my skis. One was in three pieces. The binding had been ripped off. Christian skied over and I said, 'I guess that means I'm not doing the GS.' He had been filming the run and when we watched it later I realised that he thought it was going to be a serious crash. The microphone had picked up his voice: 'Careful Alain…careful…Oh F**k!' Then it cut off as he threw the camera down. My Olympics, and a lot else besides, could have been over there and then."

Despite being in agony, Baxter went straight down and put his Slalom skis on. He wanted to know if his Games were over before they had even begun. He went free-skiing and sharp pains shot through his knee. Baxter's physio told him he had to rest for two days to have any chance of recovering enough to make the Slalom start-line. So, as his team-mates trained, Baxter recovered, watched movies and waited.

"After two days off I felt far better and trained briefly on February 22. Then I skied once on the race piste but wasn't overly enthusiastic because the conditions had changed so drastically from when we'd arrived. It was snowing and wet. It looked horrific. When we went free skiing on the hill later the conditions had changed again. It was warmer and everyone was bouncing all over the piste. I was sick, I'd done all the preparation and had been skiing well before my crash but that's skiing for you. It's the same for everyone. I felt terrible after skiing on the hill. I felt like I couldn't put two turns together. I thought, 'Here we go again.' Christian told me not to worry because everyone was the same. But it didn't make me feel any better."

When Baxter woke on February 23, the weather was overcast again. His knee ached and his sinuses were so blocked that it felt as if he was being slowly suffocated. It was not how he would have hoped to feel going into a big race. On the practice hill Baxter free skied. He practiced his positions, carved a little, but he knew that conditions on the race piste were very different so drew little confidence from the session. He'd have little time to turn that around. The clock was ticking. Baxter would be in the starting gate within the hour.

"The inspection felt different to other big races I'd been in. There was an excitement in the air but it was mixed with nerves. I put my Walkman on, something easy to listen to, and got to work. I inspected the course carefully. There was a long flat at the top, out of a hairpin and then into a big banana gate, before the pitch started. Then there was a bit of flat, another little pitch, and a side hill and then on to the finish.

"I knew every gate by heart, knew exactly where I needed to do what. Conditions were far from perfect. It almost felt a bit Scottish. I knew that a lot of people wouldn't complete the course that day. You could ski fast by carving but you'd be risking a lot, or you could lose a lot by skiing round, clean, nice and safe. That wouldn't even be an option for the later starters. By then the course would be cut up anyway. They'd have to go for it, like me. I was starting 20th. I knew that I had to aim for the top 15 in the first run. To do that I'd have to put everything on the line. The course was tough and conditions were far from ideal, but I knew that if I could nail two good runs I'd be top ten, or even on the podium. It was that sort of day."

As Baxter waited in the start area for his number to be called, he tried to clear his mind of everything but the race. He went over the course in his mind again and again. He'd travelled long and far to get to this point and he didn't want to blow it. He'd conquered his nerves. He was relaxed but would fire himself up when his time came. This was it, Baxter was on his own. It was him against the mountain, against the clock. If he got it right no-one else would matter.

Though alone in body, Baxter wasn't alone in spirit. In Aviemore, Baxter's grandparents sat glued to the television waiting for their grandson to come out of the gate. Never had they imagined he'd go quite so far in the sport. Elsewhere in the village, Ian Baxter sat on the edge of his seat, waiting to do every turn with his son. If Baxter had inherited his race pedigree from anyone it was him. In The Cairngorm Hotel, Baxter's friends huddled round the television and somewhere outside Edinburgh Baxter's mother ran the gauntlet of traffic police as she raced to reach her sister's house in time for the race. She'd booked flights to Salt Lake but couldn't find accommodation. Baxter had told her to cancel the trip and watch on TV. His mother had agreed, warning her son, 'I'll be so annoyed if you win a medal and we're not there.'

Baxter watched skier after skier disappear out of the gate. From the live feed he saw many of them crash unceremoniously. With each faller, the tension in the starter's tent mounted. These were skiers who stood on World Cup podiums week in, week out, but this was the Olympics. It was special. It was the race that reached out to the world. If you cracked under pressure you were history. If you tackled it head-on the reward was immortality, for Baxter more than most.

If any of this was going through Baxter's mind it didn't show. The Highlander gave off an air of calm. His time was coming.

"Ten seconds!" cried the starter.

He did his final warm-up, psyched himself up and was summoned to the start gate.

"5, 4, 3, 2, 1!"

Baxter was given the signal that he could go in his own time:

"Go – Partez – Los!"

He placed his poles over the baton and paused to compose his thoughts. This was it. This was what he'd worked half his life for. He took a final deep breath. Everything seemed to go quiet. Everything apart from skier and course faded into the background. Baxter rocked forward on his skis, pushed off and flew out of the start gate...

> CHAPTER 9   **THE APPEAL**

ARGUMENTS AND COUNTER-ARGUMENTS
COURT CONVENES
AWAITING THE VERDICT
THE PANEL DECIDES

9   THE APPEAL

Prior to Baxter's CAS hearing on September 5-6, Dr Bryan Finkle submitted an initial report to the IOC, which was obliged to respond with its counter-arguments. The process went on under the watchful eye of CAS. Finkle had been involved in the forensic toxicology of drug abuse in athletes for fifteen years, including ten overseeing the National Football League (NFL) anti-doping policy. He was a reliable and eminently qualified witness. Finkle's opposite number at the IOC was Professor Don Catlin, a member of the IOC Medical Commission and whose lab had conducted Baxter's test. It is said that prior to the Seoul Olympics in 1988, Catlin oversaw three failed dope-tests on sprinter Carl Lewis and a number of the US Track & Field team, though a ten day ban was the maximum sentence meted out.

ARGUMENTS AND COUNTER-ARGUMENTS

Throughout July and August, Finkle and Catlin traded arguments and scientific theory as part of the pre-hearing consultation process (a summary of which is reproduced for the first time below). Finkle's first salvo in the war of words between the two scientific heavyweights was to question the validity of the IOC's test on Baxter's sample at its laboratory at UCLA.

> *The analysis cannot be used to determine either the dose or the source of the substance found. Nor can it determine whether the substance found was in fact methamphetamine or levmetamfetamine. This is a very important distinction as only methamphetamine has significant stimulant properties. Methamphetamine and levmetamfetamine have the same molecular formula but are optical isomers. Levmet-amfetamine is to methamphetamine what a mirror image is to its object. However, the two have very different pharmacological properties.*

It is suggested (by the IOC) that levmetamfetamine is a "related substance" to methamphetamine. Scientifically it is not enough simply to say that because the two substances have the same chemical formula and molecular weight they are related in the sense needed for them to be considered a banned substance in the field of doping in sport. It is vital to consider the pharmacological activity of a substance when assessing its likelihood for abuse in sport.

There could be thousands of "related substances" if chemical similarity was enough on its own to constitute a related substance. It is not there as a simple "catch all" clause. To be related, the substance must act in an equivalent way to a banned substance. Levmetamfetamine does not have an equivalent effect to methamphetamine. Methamphetamine is a potent stimulant which is widely abused and levmetamfetamine is a nasal decongestant.

Catlin's response to Finkle's claims differed little from the stubborn view taken by the IOC in Lausanne.

This argument is fundamentally flawed for the following simple reason. The IOC Medical Commission has included methamphetamine as a Prohibited Substance. It has elected not to differentiate between the two forms and therefore the term methamphetamine must be taken to include both forms. In accordance with Article 3 of Chapter III of the Anti-Doping Code, the inclusion of a Prohibited Substance in the Code is not subject to appeal. That in itself disposes of the first limb of the Appellant's case. He is not entitled to rewrite the law to exclude his offence.

Finkle also provided the IOC with his expert view on what Baxter had ingested and how he came to have the banned substance in his system.

An alleged positive result for methamphetamine can be reported from an analysis of urine of individuals who have used US Vick's Inhaler. Studies have shown that the use of the US Vick's Inhaler produces concentrations of the drug detected in urine in the low nanogram per millilitre (ng/ml) range (Baxter had 20-25 ng/ml). This is in sharp contrast to the urine profile after use of methamphetamine in doses which cause central nervous system (CNS) stimulation. There are some reports which suggest that levmetamfetamine has some stimulant effect; however: this potency could not, particularly using a Vick's Inhaler, provide CNS stimulation and improve athletic performance.

Catlin's retort in his expert report, again varied little from the IOC's stance in Lausanne.

The Appellant contends that the positive test for methamphetamine was the result of use of a Vick's Vapor Inhaler and asserts that this appeal must proceed on this factual premise. In putting forward this premise the Appellant stumbles at the starting gate. For it is irrelevant to the constitution of a doping offence as defined by the Anti Doping Code. It is not incumbent upon the IOC to disprove alleged subjective circumstances which lead to a positive result for methamphetamine. The relevant conditions flow, rather, from the simple objective facts. A standard IOC doping test detected the presence of methamphetamine in the urine sample provided by the Appellant. Methamphetamine is listed as a prohibited substance in the Anti Doping Code. This ban cannot be the subject of an appeal pursuant to Article 3 of Chapter III. The mere presence of that prohibited substance is sufficient to constitute a doping offence. A doping offence is committed regardless of whether the athlete's performance could have benefited from the substance in question.

Finkle's opinion that Levmetamfetamine had little or no stimulant properties was backed up by Dr Kurt Weingand, principal clinical scientist at Procter & Gamble.

The compound methamphetamine exists in two chemical forms (isomers): Levo-methamphetamine (Levmetamfetamine) has pharmacological activity markedly different from that of dextro-

methamphetamine (Methamphetamine). Levmetamfetamine does not have the potent stimulant properties of methamphetamine. In one report, an oral does of 13.7mg of levmetamfetamine (up to 85 times greater than that provided by a single dose of a US Vick's Inhaler) had no stimulatory effects on the CNS of human beings.

The final thrust of Finkle's statement referred to the controversial introduction of Professor Hemmersbach as an IOC expert witness in Lausanne.

Hemmersbach was called as a witness without any written statement being provided and he produced no documents to support his opinions. He made a number of statements that I would query or disagree with if they were properly recorded. His opinion that the separation analysis is not common practice is not true. This would be standard practice if a presumptive positive urine test occurred as part of any drug abuse detection program, including athlete programs, in the US.

As the Chief Consulting Forensic Toxicologist for the NFL, I can confirm that in cases of purported methamphetamine positive tests, the laboratory will conduct further analysis to determine the presence of methamphetamine or levmetamfetamine. Furthermore, if levmetamfetamine was the substance found and results were consistent with therapeutic use of a Vick's Inhaler this would not be upheld as a doping infraction.

Catlin's standpoint was unflinching, however.

There was no need for isomer analysis because the Anti-Doping Code makes no distinction between the separate isomers of methamphetamine, namely methamphetamine and levmetamfetamine.

Finkle had also unearthed some legal precedent.

A Minnesota judge has let stand a lawsuit charging CompuChem Laboratories with negligence for reporting a drug test as positive for methamphetamine without testing for the specific isomer that would indicate illegal drug use. On April 18, 1988, Ronald Fenney was ordered to submit urine samples for drug testing. His urine sample was reported by CompuChem, a major drug testing lab, as positive for methamphetamine. Confronted with the results, Fenney claimed he had been using several over-the-counter decongestants, including a Vick's Inhaler. Fenney's suit alleges that CompuChem was negligent for reporting his test as positive without testing for the dextro isomer (methamphetamine). It should have attempted to distinguish between the legal and illegal forms of methamphetamine, the lawsuit reasons.

With each party enlightened as to what to expect at the hearing, they retired to prepare their final cases. Both Baxter, represented by Beloff and Lewis, and the IOC, represented by Jan Paulsson of Freshfields Bruckhaus Deringer, would be required to present their opening submissions before CAS, lasting no longer than 30 mins. Following the presentations, refined scientific arguments would be put forward by Finkle and Catlin. Each side would have the chance to cross-examine before Beloff and Paulsson delivered their closing oral submissions. Baxter would also be given the chance to give a brief statement if he wished. Thereafter it would be down to the three man CAS panel comprising, David Rivkin, President (nominated by CAS) and two arbitrators – Professor Richard McLaren (nominated by Baxter) and Dirk-Reiner Martens (nominated by the IOC) – to decide whether to uphold or reject the appeal. The proceedings would last two days. Baxter hoped that he would never have to see the inside of a courtroom again.

COURT CONVENES

The Court of Arbitration for Sport convened on September 5 in London's Tower 42. And so events were played out against the dramatic backdrop of the London skyline, offering Baxter some respite during breaks from the dry proceedings. As Clark recalls.

"Having the hearing in London saved us thousands of pounds in airfares that the Fund could ill afford. The tribunal ran over two days and Alain and I kept ourselves amused between sessions by monitoring the progress of the SwissRe Tower ('The Gherkin') being built alongside Tower 42. I think Alain would have rather gone to work with those guys 60 storeys up all day than sit through the hearing, but he did everything that was asked of him. Even when he was baited by the IOC he never reacted. He just sat, attentively, waiting to say his piece."

It was a huge boon to have Beloff present Baxter's case. The CAS hearing would be a more interactive affair than Lausanne – there the IOC was judge and jury – but in London Beloff was guaranteed a platform and the IOC was required to convince CAS that its actions were justifiable. Beloff's opening submission and statement of case was lengthy and peppered with legal precedent and scientific reference. The main prongs of Baxter's defence have been briefly laid out in these pages before but Beloff's statement is summarised below. He argued that:-

a) The IOC had not established that what was found in Baxter's sample was actually a prohibited substance. *(Supported by Finkle's expert opinion of the definition of Methamphetamine and Levmet-amfetamine)*

b) On proper construction of the IOC rules, it needed to establish fault in Baxter – and had failed to do so. *(Again, relying on Finkle's findings and through establishing that there was no intent on Baxter's part)*

c) Given the facts of this case, the sanction of disqualification was disproportionate. *(With reference to Swiss law and the European Convention of Human Rights)*

Beloff outlined how Baxter had come to ingest the banned substance and how the IOC had accepted his version of events. He highlighted how a simple test to prove Baxter's innocence was repeatedly refused by the IOC. Further, Beloff sought to demonstrate why Levmetamfetamine could not be considered a stimulant like Methamphetamine and that Baxter's sample had the merest trace of 'Methamphetamine', consistent only with therapeutic use of a Vick's Inhaler. Beloff directly challenged the actions of the IOC Inquiry Commission for springing a surprise witness in Lausanne, giving Lewis no opportunity to produce evidence to contradict him.

Beloff's tack altered after stating the facts of the case. He attacked the construction of the IOC Anti-Doping Code. It was this that the IOC had repeatedly hidden behind in Lausanne. To have any chance with CAS, Beloff would be required to challenge the very foundations of the IOC Code which Baxter's unique case had exposed as inconsistent. Beloff challenged article after article of the Code. He highlighted the two definitions of what constituted doping:

1. The use of an expedient which is potentially harmful to athletes' health and/or capable of enhancing performance.

2. The presence in the athlete's body of a prohibited substance.
(IOC Code, Chapter II, Article 2)

Baxter, argued Beloff, was guilty of neither. It was his belief that the IOC had not established fault in Baxter's case and thus could not disqualify him:

"Use connotes some form of deliberate act."
(Chapter I, Article 1, IOC Code, p11).

"One cannot, in ordinary parlance, 'use' a substance, of the existence of which one is unaware."

By its own Code, the IOC could not find an athlete guilty if they established that the substance was present unintentionally, argued Beloff. Compounded by the fact that the substance was neither banned, that the IOC had not done enough to prove that the substance there was actually prohibited, and that it was not performance-enhancing, it was unlawful under Swiss law, to disqualify Baxter, posed Beloff, flexing every inch of his legal muscle.

With Beloff's polished presentation complete, it fell to Paulsson to present the IOC's case. According to eyewitness accounts, Paulsson seemed unprepared and inconsistent. It took Baxter's team back to the dark days of

Lausanne when the IOC had displayed a certainty in its own procedures that bordered on arrogance. Paulsson ran through the IOC's main points but it is claimed that his presentation lacked the authority of Beloff. Even Baxter was stunned at the lacklustre performance.

"The impression I got was that the IOC lawyer was terrible. He was fumbling through the case and didn't seem very professional while Beloff had been brilliant. Someone said to me at the end of the first day, 'The IOC lawyer was awful, wasn't he?' We were surprised that they'd been so unprepared."

Baxter wasn't alone in his opinion. Friend, no stranger to a courtroom herself, was in total agreement.

"I was fairly confident that we'd given the IOC a bloody nose after the first day because they changed their argument halfway through. They came into the hearing pretty cocksure but they realised that we were running rings around them. We had our argument well and truly in order. They came back with a much stronger approach on day two."

McNeilly, who'd come to the CAS hearing in the hope of seeing Baxter draw a line under the debacle for once and for all, was also stunned to see how lackadaisical the IOC was.

"The representation of Alain's case was first class. It couldn't have been clearer or better. The IOC counsel, on the other hand, were ill-prepared. They even had flights booked to go back the first night. They thought it was going to be a walkover. After the first day they were struggling. They weren't ready for it at all. Apparently, they had to go out overnight and buy numerous reference books. We'd caught them off-guard. The IOC lawyer was extremely eminent but I don't think his client took it seriously at all."

After opening submissions and the presentation of expert witness statements, Baxter's team had scored vital points against the IOC and he left the hearing to train with every reason to be optimistic. The following morning, Paulsson was far better prepared. He looked as if he hadn't slept a wink but he finally brought something constructive to the table. He cross-examined Finkle and very much followed Catlin's lead. Beloff was then given his chance to cross-examine the IOC expert witness. Clark remembers distinctly how Beloff used all his courtroom experience on Catlin.

"Beloff was pushing Catlin for his opinion on the definition argument – are Methamphetamine and Levmetamfetamine different compounds? Why were they listed separately in numerous reference books? Didn't they have different pharmaceutical effects? Catlin refused to answer but Beloff pushed him and he said, 'All this is, is, is… stupid.' I thought then that we'd won. I felt that it wasn't the view that an expert witness should take."

When Beloff finally let Catlin off the hook, the panel asked Baxter if he had anything to add. It was the last thing he felt like doing but it was the least he owed his team. He also owed it to himself to tell his story one last time.

The Baxter Clan motto is *Vincit Veritas*: Truth Conquers/Prevails. This was very much how the honest Scot had approached his ordeal. He never tried to mislead the IOC or told an untruth. There were no smoke and mirrors, no subterfuge, he just told his story in a frank and consistent manner. There was no doubting his veracity. Again, Friend found him to be a most compelling witness.

"Alain had sat for two days and was gracious and cooperative. That clearly had an effect on the arbitrators. You immediately warmed to him. His story was from the heart. There was no attempt to blame other people. He clearly did not have a dishonest bone in his body."

McNeilly couldn't help but be moved as Baxter told his story and pleaded with the panel to acknowledge his simple mistake. This was the end of a journey for her too. She'd been with the skier through the unimaginable highs and unforeseeable lows.

"Alain's plea was absolutely heartfelt and I had tears in my eyes hearing it. Judging from the looks on the faces of the panel, I think they could see it too. You could have all the scientific arguments in the world but at the end of the day it came down to simple human error."

Baxter's plea marked the end of proceedings and the feeling among him and his team was that they'd done everything they could.

"I believed that my legal team had made the best possible presentation of my case. I thought there was a good chance I'd get my medal back and world ranking points reinstated which would have been a huge result."

Friend was in accordance:

"We knew we'd given it our best shot. We'd had a fair hearing. It was the trial Alain deserved. The panel listened to our arguments and we knew we'd given the IOC some food for thought."

AWAITING THE VERDICT

Typically, CAS would return a verdict within days. It would take over five weeks to rule on Baxter's case. With a job well-done, Baxter parted with Friend, Lewis and Beloff with a feeling of optimism. They'd all played their part. They couldn't have argued harder and Baxter's fate now lay with the arbitrators. Helpless to steer his fate, he returned to where it had all begun. Not Salt Lake, not Lausanne, but Aviemore. Where Baxter had taken his first tentative steps on skis as a two year old. Where he'd first been bitten by the skiing bug. Where he'd returned year after year as he worked his way up the rankings from an unranked teenager to 11th best in the world. Where he'd been hailed as a hero by the entire village after taking a bronze medal home from Salt Lake. Where he'd subsequently had to flee, against every instinct. Where he'd choked back the tears as he returned to the close knit village to explain, almost apologetically, why he'd never get the medal back. It was what had made him the man he was and there was nowhere else he'd rather receive the news which could sensationally return his medal, or tarnish his reputation forever.

On the morning of October 16, 2002, McNeilly and Baxter drove to Clark's house to await the outcome of the appeal. The three waited in Clark's kitchen with trepidation. The BOA would be informed of the decision by CAS at 10.30am and Clegg would call immediately after to deliver the verdict. At 10.55am, a press conference was scheduled for The Coylumbridge Hotel. There the massed ranks of the press waited. The trio made, and left untouched, repeated cups of tea. The kitchen clock seemed not to move, the second hand keeping slow time like a metronome. When the telephone rang it seemed as if everything suddenly went into fast forward. The mood in the room had been mixed – cautiously optimistic, as Clark remembers. He'll never forget the look on Baxter's face as he took the call from Clegg.

"Alain listened intently and the colour drained from his face. He looked over and made a cutting gesture across his throat. We'd lost the appeal."

Despite the obvious gloom, Clark and McNeilly had to move fast. After the grainy fax from CAS started to come through with the full verdict they had ten minutes in the car on the way to the press conference to pick out any relevant comments. Baxter sat silently in the back of the car in a daze. Despite rejecting Baxter's appeal, the verdict was the closest it could have been to a full exoneration. Baxter would never get his medal back nor his result reinstated, but CAS, deliberately or otherwise, had provided McNeilly and Clark with the tools with which to mount a massive damage limitation exercise on Baxter's unfairly tainted reputation.

(A summary of the release is below).

CAS – Arbitral Award
Between – Mr Alain Baxter & IOC

Findings
There is no dispute as to the circumstances of Mr Baxter's use of the Vick's Inhaler and his ingestion of levmetamfetamine. The level of substance found in his body is consistent with his taking the medication for therapeutic use. The IOC has not sought to present any evidence disputing Mr Baxter's description of the circumstances of his taking of the medication. The Panel finds Mr Baxter's story to be sincere and compelling. At the levels found in Mr Baxter's body it is very unlikely that the levmetamfetamine had any stimulant effect.

Whether or not Mr Baxter should have been more careful before taking the medication is irrelevant to our decision. Consistent CAS case law has held that athletes are strictly responsible for substances they place in their body and that for purposes of disqualification neither intent nor negligence needs to be proven by the sanctioning body.

Verdict
The Panel is not without sympathy for Mr Baxter who appears to be a sincere and honest man who did not intend to obtain a competitive advantage in the race. Nevertheless, because Mr Baxter took the medication, at the time of the slalom race his body contained a prohibited substance. The consequence for this must be disqualification and the loss of his medal.

In light of the consequences already suffered, the Panel does not believe that it would be appropriate for him to have to reimburse the IOC for its costs of this proceeding.

Recommendations

The panel notes that for apparent greater clarity the 27 September 2002 draft version of the WADA code expressly indicates that both L- and D- isomers of all stimulants are prohibited substances.

The IOC may wish to consider at some time whether to distinguish between the two isomers of methamphetamine and to introduce a threshold as it has done in the case of other stimulants, such as caffeine.

There were many positives to be taken from the verdict. Particularly that CAS praised Baxter's character and cleared him of any intent to cheat. There was also a victory of sorts that would have wide-ranging benefits for other athletes in the future. Friend spoke of giving the IOC a 'bloody nose'. CAS had taken note, suggesting that it distinguish between the two isomers of methamphetamine and introduce a threshold. Subsequent to Baxter's case the IOC amended its Code, a change that is also reflected in the WADA (World Anti-Doping Agency) Code. It was a considerable coup to force such a change in policy. It wouldn't bring Baxter's medal back but it was as good as an admission that the Code had been perilously ambiguous before.

It only remained for Baxter to face the press one last time. McNeilly had already prepared two press releases: one anticipating really good news; the other anticipating moderately good news. She couldn't bring herself to pen the press release imagining that CAS would damn Baxter and throw out his appeal.

"The verdict wasn't what we wanted but it was littered with complimentary quotes about Alain. It had been as good a result as we could have hoped for, if I'm honest. We read out the highlights from the verdict at the press conference but Alain didn't really say much. I think he was fed up with the whole thing and wanted to get on with his life. We all did. After the press conference I was lost. John and I didn't know what to do with ourselves. The appeal had been our lives for six months."

A part of the ruling which had gone virtually unnoticed in the heat of the moment was actually of huge significance. CAS had ruled that Baxter was not required to cover the costs of the IOC. That was something which could have bankrupted him. As it was, the cost of the appeal ran into tens of thousands of pounds, even though the team had billed for only a tiny fraction of what they were due. Finkle invoiced for $10,000 but said that he would accept half that amount because he believed wholeheartedly in the skier. Blackstone Chambers billed for a mere fraction of the true value of the services of Beloff and Lewis. The BOA held to its part of the deal and did not ask for any recompense for Friend's considerable time in the previous six months. The Appeal Fund would almost, but not totally, cover the costs of the appeal but this was the last thing on Baxter's mind.

"We'd lost on paper but CAS's comments and recommendations made it worth it in the end. I wouldn't benefit, but at least others would. It was also vindication for all the hard work John and my lawyers had put in. Having it officially said that I had not intended to cheat or gained any competitive advantage was brilliant. The way people were speaking to me before, I felt like I'd been cleared already. But there was a minority of people who'd shout, 'Cheat' at me in the street. The CAS decision cleared it up for once and for all."

When the dust from the press conference settled, Clark reminded Baxter of Bill Taylor's offer to take the case to the European Court of Civil Rights. Taylor called CAS's decision 'utterly perverse'. Baxter had already made up his mind, however. It was over. He'd taken it as far as he could. His friends, family, the press, the public, and his fellow skiers all believed he was innocent. CAS had said as much. That was all that mattered. He wanted to put it behind him and get back to doing what he did best. In the heat of the moment, Clark found it hard to digest.

"It was difficult to accept Alain's decision because there were still a lot of people, myself included, who wanted to push on and fight it. But it is his career, his medal, so we had to let it go. It was important to respect that. Alain just wanted to get back racing."

In the aftermath of the appeal, Baxter's legal team was philosophical. They'd been realistic in their chances of overturning the IOC's decision. Friend knew that it was the most powerful organisation in sport and challenging its statutes was always going to be a long shot. As with the IOC Inquiry Commission, Friend was able to speak informally to members of CAS after the hearing and was left in no doubt that the decision was a close call.

"I believe, and I think by reading between the lines of the written decision, that CAS deliberated long and hard to see if it could open the door for Alain to get his medal back, and then shut it smartly behind him, but I knew how hard that would have been for them. Had Alain won the appeal, the ramifications for the IOC and the global anti-doping laws would have been huge. It could have thrown doubt over some previous cases and potentially exposed the IOC, many international sporting federations and national governing bodies to a Pandora's box of claims for huge damages."

In any case, the fall-out from Baxter's failed appeal was considerable. Clark decided to bring an end to a 25 year career in skiing, so disgusted was he with the outcome.

"In all the years I've worked in sport I've been trained to put the athlete at the centre of everything. I was taught that it was wrong to put the needs of the organisation before the athlete. This is what turned me off the sport I loved. I always thought that the Olympics were about the athletes, but it's about protecting the brand. The modern Olympic movement was supposed to be about sportsmanship, about fulfilling dreams, with the athletes as kings. The IOC had blown that founding principle out of the water. Its Anti-Doping Code went against this dictum, using a testing system based upon the presumption of guilt."

In the wake of Baxter's case, the British government commissioned an independent report into doping in sport. The report highlighted Baxter's case, focusing in particular on how it had been possible for him to innocently ingest a banned substance while under the impression that he was using a product repeatedly cleared for use by his team doctor. To underline the danger, it drew up a list of other common over-the-counter remedies and near identical products containing banned substances.

Permitted	*Banned*
Alka Seltzer	Alka Seltzer XL
Beechams Lemon Tablets	Beechams Hot Lemon
Hedex	Hedex Extra

Resolve	Resolve Extra
Solpadine Max	Solpadine
Lemsip (Ireland)	Lemsip (NI & UK)
Night Nurse	Day Nurse

Baxter's family rallied round to support him after the CAS decision. They closed ranks. It was time to reclaim their relative from the public eye. It was time for the journalists and the television vans to leave the village. Life was to return to normal for the first time in nine months. They were all angered by the decision, despite the sugar-coating it had been given.

"CAS said he was not a cheat. If he is not a cheat, what is he?" said Baxter's grandfather.

Lesley McKenna saw the wider issues raised by Baxter's case. She was an athlete, like him, and subject to the rules laid down by FIS, the IOC and WADA.

"What happened to Alain was ridiculous, it was wrong, and I was dying to wade in on his behalf. But what could I have done? Of course cheating is bad. Nothing enrages me more and Alain feels exactly the same. It would never cross his mind after all the work he has put in to get to the top of the sport. An IOC spokesman said at the time that he didn't believe that any elite athlete has never thought about taking performance enhancing drugs. You would have to be dishonest to make a statement like that, and they transfer it onto athletes like Alain. It's an insult. When the general public hear statements like that they think that athletes just want to win a medal at all costs."

Baxter's father, too, took issue with how the IOC had conducted itself:

"I think the IOC jumped the gun by awarding the medal to Raich so soon. If they had waited I think that when the whole thing settled down they may have given it back. I think the IOC could have done more than it did, especially after CAS said he hadn't cheated."

There was precedent for Olympic medals being returned retrospectively. Cases were thin on the ground, but it proved that the IOC was capable of being more flexible than it had been with Baxter. After a judging scandal in the ice skating at Salt Lake, instead of retracting the gold medal awarded to Russian couple Elena Berezhnaya and Anton Sikharulidze, who had unwittingly benefited from some unscrupulous judging, and giving it to

Canadians Jamie Salé and David Pelletier, who had only won silver as a result, the IOC awarded a second gold. At the previous Olympics in Nagano, snowboarder Ross Rebagliati of Canada had been stripped of his gold medal after a positive test for Cannabis only to have it returned when he argued that he'd ingested the drug passively from friends. Farther back in history, in 1912, Jim Thorpe, a Native American, had his two gold medals for Decathlon and Pentathlon taken away because he'd once been paid $2 to play in a baseball game and was thus a 'professional'. After a 1983 film (*The Man of Bronze*) brought it to the attention of a wider American public, Thorpe's medals were returned to his family.

THE OTHER MEDAL WINNER

There was no such happy ending for Baxter. Despite Raich repeatedly stating that he did not want Baxter's medal, which he believed the Scot had won fairly, the Austrian was awarded the bronze medal for the 2002 Men's Olympic Slalom. Raich had only accepted it after he and Baxter met back on the piste in the 2002/03 season and discussed the matter. Before receiving the medal in a low key ceremony in Vienna in December 2002, Raich said:

"Alain told me it wasn't my mistake so I should accept the medal. That's what I shall do."

They were rivals and friends but also victims of circumstance and Baxter had graciously insisted that Raich accept the medal.

"After my first race back Benni came up to me and said, 'I'm sorry that they want to give me the medal.' I said, 'Don't worry about it. I was disqualified. It's not your fault. It's yours.' I don't blame him for not giving it back. I don't know what I would do in the same situation but it was his choice."

Raich was reluctant to accept the meaningless token of someone else's success but he would have entered a whole new storm of controversy to refuse it. There were rumours that he was going to return it to Baxter but it never happened. It didn't stop other skiers hypothesising what they might have done if they'd been in Raich's position. A number of top racers, such as Killian Albrecht, were in no doubt as to what they would have done.

"If I was Raich I would have given Baxter the medal right back."

If there is a happy ending to this terrible series of events it occurred in February 2003, a matter of weeks after Raich took receipt of the medal. Baxter's mother had made an emotional journey to the World Championship in St Moritz. It was the first time she'd watch her son race since Salt Lake. It was a poignant moment and she brimmed with pride.

"There were eight of us there to support Alain. We walked up early so that we could get a good spot where we could see most of the course. We had big Scottish flags and a banner that we wanted Alain to see too. It soon got very busy and another group pushed their way alongside us. We were trying to stand our ground because we'd been there for ages. A young girl in the group kept looking over at us and I felt a bit self-conscious but thought nothing of it. After some time she pushed past some people and said to me, 'Are you Alain Baxter fans?' I thought it seemed obvious but I said, 'Yes, actually I'm his mother.' As soon as I'd said that she said, 'I must introduce you to my mother. I'm Benjamin Raich's sister.' The whole Raich family was standing next to us.

"Raich's mother came over to us but she couldn't speak any English at all. I don't speak any German either so her daughter translated for us. She said, 'We're all so sorry. It's terrible what happened to Alain. Benjamin didn't want to take the medal at all. He knows that he didn't win it on the hill but the government put pressure on him to take it to improve the team's medal tally. We all thought that Alain should have kept the medal.'"

As the mothers of the two skiers embraced, everything that had gone before seemed to disappear. All the hurt that Sue Dickson had bottled up inside flowed out. Only another mother could understand the heartbreak, the helplessness that Baxter's mother had felt watching the son she'd nurtured suffer so much, lose something which was so precious. To hear the words that she knew were true all along, that her son had won his medal fairly, that it had shamed one of his great rivals to take the hollow trophy, brought a humanity to the situation that the IOC had refused to acknowledge. Baxter, Raich and their families had been thrown together by fate and had made their peace. It only remained for the self-serving dinosaurs who ran the IOC to come to terms with the hurt they'd caused, to the wounds that might never heal. To many it seemed that they'd used Baxter to re-establish the integrity of an organisation brought to its knees by internal corruption. All they'd actually succeeded in doing was devaluing the IOC brand further and destroying the dream that a child had held as long as he could remember. Baron Pierre de Coubertin, founder of the modern Olympic movement, would have been turning in his grave.

> CHAPTER 10   **MOVING ON**

BACK ON THE PISTE
SEASON 2003/04
SEASON 2004/05
APPEARING ON SUPERSTARS
LOOKING TO THE FUTURE

10   **MOVING ON**

There was much fall-out from Baxter's painful ordeal at the hands of the IOC. His very existence as a skier was threatened after UK Sport pulled its funding due to Baxter being rendered ineligible from future selection to the Olympic team under a BOA bye-law.

It would take another appeal, this time to the BOA, by Clark and McNeilly, to have Baxter's eligibility for selection for the 2006 Olympic Games, and thus his Talented Athlete Programme funding, restored. It would be near the end of his first season back before it was eventually all ironed out. Another appeal was the last thing Baxter wanted but £70,000 per year was at stake and, more importantly, the benefits (to the whole team) of Baxter's trainer, physio and serviceman. It was worth fighting for if only to help his young team-mates fulfil their Olympic dreams four years later.

Baxter had to come to terms with his recalculated world ranking too. It had taken a battering. Had Baxter not lost his ranking points from the medal-winning performance, he would probably have started the 2002/03 season ranked 18th, if not better. Not only had he been denied the valuable ranking points that the podium finish had brought, he had missed numerous races at the end of the season, not least the World Cup Finals. As Baxter was improving with every race it is not inconceivable that he could have bettered his record-breaking 4th place at the 2000/01 finals, especially after the massive confidence boost of being on the Olympic podium. For Baxter to start his first race of the year ranked 43 smacked of injustice.

BACK ON THE PISTE

But Baxter was ecstatic to be back on the piste and beat Benjamin Raich into 3rd place in his first race back at Loveland Pass, Colorado, echoing his result at Salt Lake. More ironic was the fact that the first two World Cup races of the

2002/03 season were to be held at Deer Valley on the same piste as the 2002 Olympics. After enjoying a brief hiatus from the press attention which had dogged him for months, Baxter was front page news again as the press painted a picture of the skier returning to the scene of his greatest result to avenge the IOC.

"When we arrived, the press were everywhere and wouldn't leave me alone. I'd foolishly agreed to do a video diary for *Ski Sunday* too. It seemed like everyone was building me up for a podium finish. I thought they might have lost interest in me by then, but I realised that the press are always going to prick up their ears when I have a good result. I decided there and then that I'd have to learn to live with it."

It had been a long road back to the World Cup start-line. It was a sight that, at some stages during the summer, he thought he would never see. Baxter felt strangely unmoved to be back. He didn't feel the excitement of the occasion or any discernable nerves. It felt comfortable. It was where he belonged. However, it wouldn't be the triumphant return that the press and so many fans, new and old, had wished for. Baxter straddled in the first race and did not qualify in the second. And to the great shame of the IOC, it would

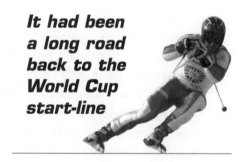

It had been a long road back to the World Cup start-line

set the template for Baxter for the next three seasons. From a period of almost consistent improvement up to 2002, Baxter would enter the most frustrating spell of his career. He'd never recapture the form of Salt Lake or of his breakthrough season in 2000/01. Despite skiing consistently well in practice and breaking new ground by winning his first Europa Cup races, Baxter would struggle in World Cups. It was the scenario that many had dreaded. John Clark had seen Baxter shrug off psychological setback after setback but knew that there'd be a risk that it could come back to haunt him. Baxter had put heart and soul into saving his career only to find that the emotional baggage seemed to somehow hamper his progress on the piste.

"After all that Alain had gone through I really hoped he was as unaffected as he said he was. Because it takes absolutely nothing to put you out of your stride in Slalom. If you stand at the top of the piste and feel anything less than bullet-proof you're in trouble."

Baxter stumbled through the 2002/03 season. Though he skied well in second tier events, he failed to qualify or crashed out in eight out of ten World Cups. The two races he completed, he came 11th and 14th. It was crushing for Baxter, especially as he knew that he was still capable of knocking on the door of the top ten. Yet he couldn't get it right. If he skied conservatively in an effort to make sure he completed the course, he'd be too slow to qualify. If he tried to ski faster, he would straddle.

"I couldn't attribute the straddling at all and it completely dented my confidence. I'm not sure if I'd put that down to things that had happened being in the back of my mind or the pressure on me to do well. I felt very relaxed at the start of each race and didn't feel I was putting extra pressure on myself at all."

The World Cup was the stage where he had to compete, where he'd worked so hard to establish himself. If he wasn't up there with the best there was no point in continuing with the sport. But he was skiing well and beating better ranked skiers easily on the training hill. He hoped it would only be a matter of time before his 'race pace' returned. Baxter's ranking actually improved from 43 to 31 in his first season back, a reflection that had he not missed the end of the previous season, he would be sitting even prettier. But he was left wondering why he could not consistently reproduce his best form. Detractors were already commenting that if one were to exclude his two stand-out seasons that Baxter's progress was steady and excellent by any standards. But that wasn't enough for Baxter. He didn't want his two best seasons to be viewed as a freak occurrence, as a blip. He viewed them as very much part of his curve of improvement and wanted to continue that trajectory. He was a born competitor. He'd tasted success and he wasn't content with just making up the numbers.

But that was exactly what he was destined to do for the next two seasons. Baxter's World Cup results from the 2003/04 and 2004/05 seasons would be as indifferent as the past season. Aside from finishing 16th in the 2005 World Championships in Bormio, Italy, equalling his career-best and reminding the Scot that he could still rise to the occasion, there'd be few highlights:

SEASON: 2003/04

World Ranking: 31

DNQ1	Soelden, Austria
DNQ1	Park City, Utah
11th	Madonna, Italy
18th	Flachau, Austria
27th	Chamonix, France
19th	Wengen, Austria
DNF2	Kitzbuehel, Austria
DSQ1	Schladming, Austria
DNF1	Adelboden, Austria
12th	St Anton, Austria
25th	Kranjska Gora, Slovenia

SEASON: 2004/05

World Ranking: 40

DNF1	Beaver Creek, USA
DNQ1	Sestriere, Italy
DNQ1	Flachau, Austria
27th	Chamonix, France
DNQ1	Wengen, Austria
DNQ1	Kitzbuehel, Austria
DNF1	Schladming, Austria
DNQ2	Kranjska Gora, Slovenia

It's not unusual for Slalom skiers to suffer indifferent form. Baxter had done so throughout his career. Rarely did a season pass where he didn't suffer a dip in form or some small crisis in confidence. But he wasn't alone in this. Baxter's close friend, Kalle Palander, took the World Championship by storm in February 1999, winning the Slalom, yet didn't win another top-flight race

again until January 2003. Jean-Pierre Vidal was ranked in the top three after winning the Slalom at Salt Lake but two years later was ranked 26 in the world. Sebastian Amiez, who also shared the Salt Lake podium, was ranked 10th in the world at the time but is now ranked in the high 70s. But by his own admission, Baxter's noticeable slump in form is apparently non-attributable. Whereas in the past Baxter could look at technique or equipment for answers to his poor performance, now he was at a loss to say why he wasn't hitting the high notes.

"I can't say if my form since then has anything to do with what I went through in 2002. All I know is that I can still ski fast, fast enough to win races, and if I couldn't I probably wouldn't still be doing it. It's very frustrating and has been like this for a couple of years."

Baxter would need to look into himself to find the answers. It was clear that above all else he was subconsciously affected by his ordeal. He'd battled through it at the time using every survival mechanism in the book, but he would have had to be superhuman not to have been affected at some level.

Baxter will talk openly about his experiences at the hands of the IOC. He is sanguine about it, will joke darkly about the whole thing, but he will, if pressed, admit that it was the biggest single setback in his career. Worse than that, it was something that he had no control over. In the past when he'd been faced with a lack of funding, he'd solve it. He'd get a job. If his skis weren't feeling right he'd go back to the manufacturer and suggest some changes. Every hurdle he faced was tangible. But what happened after Salt Lake was different. Baxter said after the CAS verdict:

"It was my mistake and I just have to live with that."

It was only in the following years that he understood just what that took. Baxter is nothing if not honest. He doesn't try and hide from the fact that he's been struggling since Salt Lake. It is unavoidable. But he treats the subconscious effects of losing his medal like any other problem. He is prepared to tackle it head-on. To him it is something to be overcome with hard work, with a positive attitude, over a period of time. He is driven on by the fact that he truly believes that he can make it to the top of the sport again when he clears this final hurdle. If he can overcome this, he will be able to overcome anything the sport can throw at him.

"You can't dwell on these things. It would have been great to come out after the Olympics and win lots of races but it didn't happen, I struggled, but you get on with it. I have been having problems. I don't consciously do it. It's a mental block. However, I have had problems before and overcame them so I need to overcome this too. I've struggled for the last three years. It's been tough. There've been spots of brilliance and spots of absolute rubbish. It's up and down and I have to keep working on it."

No-one who knows Baxter doubts that he will conquer this latest challenge. No matter if he did actually improve his ranking the season after Salt Lake, despite feeling as if he had lost his form; or if the season after it would have improved again but for a late season blip; or that his biggest slide down the rankings in recent times, in the 2004/05 season, was because it was cut short through injury and dogged by equipment problems: none of this matters because, deep down inside, Baxter knows that he has to be ranked in the top ten to fulfil his god-given talent.

And so to the present. In 2005 Baxter underwent the first surgery of his career, on the knee, and has been reinvigorated by the break. It is thought the injury was caused by the training crash in Salt Lake in 2002. Baxter has switched to a new ski supplier, signed-up by the man who gave him his first set of sponsored skis as a 14-year-old, and is more excited by the 2005/06 season than any other in memory. The time away from skiing has given him time to slay some of the demons of Salt Lake. Baxter has seen a sports psychologist, though focused more on any personal problems that may be affecting his skiing rather than the medal loss *per se*. It has all left him feeling far more robust and ready for the season ahead. He feels rehabilitated.

Baxter's image, too, has been rehabilitated during the last three years. Though he has accepted that his will be the first phone to ring when a high profile athlete becomes embroiled in a drugs scandal (read Rio Ferdinand and Dwain Chambers), his reputation is beyond question.

He could hold his head up high and shrug off the stigma

Many took their lead from CAS's comments about Baxter's character, others from a gut instinct that the Scot was an innocent victim. Invitations to The Queen's summer garden party; Baxter's involvement with campaigns to get more children interested in skiing; his winning of the 2002 Pery Medal, an award from the Ski Club of Great Britain to the skier or snowboarder of any nationality for an outstanding contribution to competitive international skiing – were all massive endorsements of his character. But none more so than the invitation for Baxter to appear on *Blue Peter*, in March 2003, and on the BBC primetime show, *Superstars*. They proved to Baxter that he could hold his head up high and shrug off the stigma of being called a 'cheat'.

APPEARING ON SUPERSTARS

Baxter's appearance on Superstars was the most intriguing. He would have been right to feel apprehensive about the reception he'd receive from his fellow competitors from athletics, cycling and swimming. They are sports where doping is rife and competitors, like Olympic 400m silver-medallist Jamie Baulch, have little time for cheats. What must he have made of the little-

Moving On

known British medallist most famous for losing, not winning, an Olympic medal?

"I'd never met Alain before *Superstars*, though I knew of him. Of course the scandal did put a bit of doubt in my mind but after meeting him I could tell straight away that he was not a cheat. It's upsetting that the scandal is what he's known for, because he's a winner, a great athlete and a great man who deserves a lot more recognition for what he has achieved."

Baulch was not alone in his admiration for Baxter. By all accounts the assembled group, including Olympic gold medal winners Steve Williams (Rowing), Jason Queally (Cycling) and Marlon Devonish (Athletics) viewed the Scot as a kindred spirit. No-one had known what to expect from Baxter in the competition, but one thing that was clearly on everyone's mind was Baxter's medal. It was the first time that he'd really spent any time with Olympic medal winners from other sports and, inevitably, the subject of his medal loss did arise after a couple of drinks. The group was exclusive in that they were all Olympic medal winners. But Baxter was the rarest of all – he'd been stripped of his. Baulch was particularly disturbed by the details of Baxter's case.

"I just can't get my head around what happened to Alain. I wouldn't even like to think about losing my own Olympic medal. It must be tragic and I doubt he'll ever really come to terms with it, but at the same time when he puts his head on the pillow at night he knows he's a winner. He's got nothing to answer for. I'd defend him to anyone and that's not something I'd do lightly. There are lots of unpleasant people in sport and after meeting Alain I was thinking, 'Why couldn't this have happened to one of them?' Alain's one of the good guys."

The assembled group were united in support for Baxter but it didn't detract from the fierce rivalry. There'd be no quarter given or taken in the celebrity multi-sport competition. It was to be expected from a field of such high achievers. There were those who took the competition very seriously and there were those, like Baxter, who approached it in a more light-hearted manner. The Scot enjoyed the social aspect of the competition and would be last to bed but would wake bright-eyed and bushy-tailed ready to wipe the floor with the veritable Who's Who of British sport. It endeared him to some, like Baulch, while others hated being beaten by anyone, let alone a skier.

"What I liked best about Alain was that he wanted to do well but have fun too. That's very similar to my outlook on sport. He was good at almost everything but if there was something he couldn't do you could see that it bothered him. Only for a minute though. After that he'd give you a wink and have a laugh at himself. I couldn't believe how drunk we'd get in the evenings and then how well he'd do the next morning. There were some serious athletes there and it annoyed them to see Alain partying so hard and still beating them all hands down."

Winning the second series of *Superstars* was the best bit of public relations possible for Baxter and British skiing. It was the first time the public could compare Baxter to other top athletes and it opened people's eyes to the dedication and conditioning required to ski at the top level. The programme portrayed Baxter in a true light. He is determined and highly competitive but, more importantly, modest in victory. He combines the dedication to training of an Olympic rower with the skill and precision of a Formula 1 driver, yet is free of the ego and arrogance so often associated with individual athletes. His down-to-earth approach epitomises good sportsmanship. The experience was an eye-opener for Baxter. To be in such close proximity with so many sporting greats was humbling. Despite winning the competition, he felt as if he was back as a child at his first international race, in respectful awe of the assembled talent.

"It was great to win but look at what the other competitors have achieved in their careers. I was grateful to have even been invited. There were multiple Olympic medallists there, repeat World Champions, it was an honour to share a stage with these guys. I left wishing I was as good at my sport as they all were."

Baxter's story is an interesting one. He battled seemingly insurmountable odds to achieve what no other Briton has. He is a one-off and may be the last home-grown world class British skier for many years. He was born at a time when there'd never been so much snow in Scotland and when the slopes had never been so accessible. He was born with a natural talent into a family who lived to ski. He was blessed with an unerring determination and burning ambition and came through all the bad times in the British ski scene to be the last man standing.

His perseverance and his insistence that the Federation match his own ambitions have served to radically overhaul the sport in this country. In doing so he has simplified the landscape for up-and-coming young British skiers. Never before has the sport been better supported. Had Baxter been born into the current climate it's hard to imagine what he might have gone on to achieve. But maybe the struggle was what made the man. Nothing came easy to the Scot. He had to fight for every hour on the snow and that fight is what makes his story so special. People have to look beyond Salt Lake. To have his career interminably linked to that scandal is to do the Scot the greatest injustice. One must look at his sixteen years of near constant improvement, at the ground he has broken for aspiring British skiers, at the work he does to get more children involved in the sport, and at his role in helping move the sport as a whole forward.

Baxter would never dream of being anywhere else

LOOKING TO THE FUTURE

But Baxter's story is not at its end. He will be 32 on December 26, 2005, and considering his exceptional physical condition, should have three or four more good seasons in him. And he fully intends to go out with a bang.

"I intend to finish my career on a high. I'd like to win a World Cup and go back to the Finals. The Olympics and World Championships are where the big medals are up for grabs but the World Cup is the true test for a skier. There's not the same pressure as the Olympics or World Champs, but there are more competitors. There's ten Austrians instead of four in the Olympics. The same with Swiss, French, American, Norwegian… It would be massive to win a World Cup race, let alone the final, but I've been 4/10ths of a second from winning in the past and anything is possible. Salt Lake taught me that."

In many people's eyes the only true retribution for Baxter would be served by his winning a medal at the 2006 Winter Olympics in Turin. Work on that goal starts now. Baxter must reduce his ranking enough so that he'll

Moving On

receive a good enough start number to challenge for the podium. Baxter admits that a medal would be nice but he's not pinning his hopes on it. Before he even gets to the start gate in Italy, on February 25, 2006, Baxter will face a barrage of press attention. This will only intensify as the Games near and newspapers inevitably hail Baxter's final Games as an attempt to rewrite the history books and snatch back his medal from the grasp of the IOC.

McNeilly, for one, is worried about how Baxter will handle the pressure.

"I'm a bit concerned for him going into Turin. There'll be a lot of press attention, a lot of naïve questions put to him and he'll have to deal with it. It might have been better if he never went to another Olympics. My real hope is that he's not sitting in The Cairngorm Hotel in 30 years time telling people how he lost his bronze medal. That's my nightmare scenario."

Missing Turin 2006 was never a consideration for Baxter. He was required to make it a goal to satisfy funding requirements but, more importantly, he is a born competitor and his will to win is far greater than any grudge he might hold against the IOC. In the aftermath of Baxter's ordeal, many of his fellow skiers berated the IOC and belittled the significance of the Olympics to the skiing community, but Baxter was never drawn on the subject. When February 2006 comes round, and the top racers head for Turin, Baxter would never dream of being anywhere else. It's the stage he thrives upon and where he's proven that he can succeed.

McKenna, who will compete in Turin too, knows her cousin like no-one else. She's seen him grow from a small, shy child to an aggressive, world-beating skier, while retaining a modesty rare in the sport. She believes Baxter's story should serve as an inspiration to us all:

"It's a fairytale really. It's a positive story about overcoming obstacles and staring so-called failure in the face and realising that it was not failure but another hurdle to overcome in pursuit of your dream. Alain was never scared that it might not work. He knew there was only the smallest chance that he would succeed. He knew that what he wanted to do was going to be a long slog. Success wasn't going to come overnight so he had to realise that for a long time his life was going to be about the getting there, getting to the top of the sport. That's what saved Alain. Salt Lake was just one small step in a 20 year struggle to get to that spot. He hadn't turned up out of the blue to cause an upset. You have to look at how he kept improving, how he'd come to be standing on that piste with a genuine chance of taking home a medal."

And Baxter could quite conceivably find himself in the same position come February 2006. It's not about drawing a line under Salt Lake. With the exception of a handful of aged politicians in Lausanne, the skier is, and always will be, 'Alain Baxter, Olympic Bronze Medallist'. It is about the next step on the remarkable journey taken by a young Scottish boy who dared to realise his wildest dreams.

"Winning an Olympic medal was more than I had ever imagined I'd achieve when I set out to become a racer. After being stripped of that, Turin 2006 was never the most important race for me to go back and do. I wasn't even thinking about it in Lausanne or when the appeal was ongoing. But I'm a racer. That's what I do, it's my job.

"I'm in the sport to win. I shouldn't be in the sport if I don't want to do that. When I go to Turin of course I'm going to try and bring back a medal. It won't be easy for me but it would be sweet justice if I ended up on the podium again. But there's no guarantee so there's no point fixating on it. In the run up to the Games anything can happen. Look at my fall at Salt Lake. That could have ended my career, let alone my hopes of a medal.

"The Olympics are a lottery, a place where your worse nightmares become reality or your greatest dreams come true. Anyone who steps up to the plate on the day can win – and that includes me."

Other titles from
Dewi Lewis Media

RAFA BENÍTEZ

the authorised biography
by Paco Lloret

£12.99 softback
224 pages
ISBN: 0-9546843-7-0

On May 25th 2005, Liverpool FC won the Champions League Final in one of the most memorable and extraordinary nights of English football.

This authorised biography of the Liverpool manager is a vivid and lively account of both his personal and professional life, from childhood right through to his current achievements with Liverpool. A talented footballer, Rafa Benítez progressed through the ranks of the Real Madrid youth teams before suffering a serious injury which destroyed his dream of playing at the top of European football. Instead he had to settle for a modest playing career in the lower divisions, but still determined to achieve success in the game he became a coach, initially with Real Madrid's youth teams. Later, as a manager, he took Extremadura and Tenerife to the Spanish first division, before moving to Valencia where he won two League titles and the UEFA Cup. When Liverpool appointed him in June 2004 it was against stiff competition from three other major European clubs.

Lloret gives a real insight into what motivates Benítez, his attention to detail, his man-mangement skills, his sharp football mind and his constant quest to develop the skills of himself and his players. We also discover the steely determination with which he faced his early setbacks, his personal trauma at the tragic death of his brother-in-law, his public anger after the Madrid bombings, and the complex intrigue at Valencia which led to his move to Liverpool.

Paco Lloret has been a sports journalist for over twenty years. He first met Benítez through a mutual friend, journalist Emilio García Carrasco, and this has given him a privileged position from which to explore the personality and achievements of the manager who led Liverpool to European glory in the Champions League.

JOSÉ MOURINHO
MADE IN PORTUGAL

the authorised biography
by Luís Lourenço

£12.99 softback
224 pages
ISBN: 0-9546843-3-8

José Mourinho arrived in London in the summer of 2004. The Chelsea manager made an immediate, and at times controversial, impact on English football, with his unmistakeable self-confidence, drive and ambition.

This fascinating book charts his rise from relatively humble beginnings as assistant coach to Sir Bobby Robson, to become the most sought-after club manager in Europe.

Readers of this fascinating book will gain an insight into Mourinho's management skills, as well as his whole footballing philosophy, and his approach to motivating his players. Mourinho himself writes of his move to Roman Abramovich's Chelsea and of approaches by other clubs; his 'mind games' with Sir Alex Ferguson as Manchester United are knocked out of Europe; and his fears for his personal safety and that of his family after receiving a death threat on the eve of what should have been the biggest night of his life.

Long-term family friend, Portuguese journalist Luís Lourenço guides us through the formative years in Mourinho's coaching career, as he returns to Portugal from Barcelona at the turn of the millennium and embarks on the remarkable four-year journey which will lead him to Chelsea. A journey which includes short-lived yet turbulent spells at Portuguese giants Benfica and minnows União de Leiria, and culminates in a night of unforgettable glory for FC Porto and José Mourinho as they are crowned Champions of Europe.

www.dewilewismedia.com

For full details of all our titles
please visit our website at

www.dewilewismedia.com